Bright Beat the Water

Bright Beat the Water

Memories of a Wilderness Artist

written and illustrated by John L. Peyton

The McDonald & Woodward Publishing Company
Blacksburg, Virginia
1993

The McDonald & Woodward Publishing Company
P. O. Box 10308, Blacksburg, Virginia 24060-0308

Bright Beat the Water
Memories of a Wilderness Artist

©1993 by The McDonald & Woodward Publishing Company

All rights reserved. First printing, 1993.
Printed in the United States of America
by Braun-Brumfield, Inc., Ann Arbor, Michigan, USA

99 98 97 96 95 94 93   10 9 8 7 6 5 4 3 2 1

Library of Congress Cataloging-in-Publication Data

Peyton, John L., 1907 –
    Bright beat the water : memories of a wilderness artist / written and
  illustrated by John L. Peyton.
      p.   cm.
    ISBN 0-939923-30-0 : $14.95
      1. Peyton, John L., 1907- --Biography. 2. Authors. American—20th
  century—Biography. 3. Artists—United States—Biography. 4. Wilderness areas
  in art.
    I. Title.
PS3566.E982Z463 1993
818'.5403--dc20
[B]   93-24054
                                                                                                                                    CIP

The author gratefully acknowledges permission to quote copyrighted passages from the following works: Joanne Hart, *Witch Tree*, Holy Cow! Press, Duluth, Minnesota, 1992; and Eino Friberg (translater), *The Kalevala*, Octava Publishing Company, Helskinki, Finland, 1988.

Reproduction or translation of any part of this work, except for short excerpts used in reviews, without the written permission of the copyright owner is unlawful. Requests for permission to reproduce parts of this work, or for additional information, should be addressed to the publisher.

Contents

Preface vii

1. The View from the Hill 1
2. Haunted Cavern 9
3. La Belle Riviere 14
4. The City and the Lake 20
5. Chink 26
6. Indians 32
7. Third River 38
8. Friends 43
9. Crime and Punishment 46
10. Plunder 49
11. The Galleys of Venice 57
12. Waters of Academe 63
13. Singing in the Wilderness 69
14. Banking and Birthing 77
15. Timber Farm 83
16. Portages 89
17. The Female of the Species 98
18. A Winter's Tale 107
19. Insects in the Impasto 117
20. Word Wrassler 126
21. Don't Go near the Water 132

22. Meetings with Mukwa 139
23. In the Cradle of the Deep 150
24. Spirits beneath the Ice 156
25. Beware the Oriniac 164
26. The Once and Future Queen 172
27. Riding the Turtle 178
28. Seas and Shores of 'Tschgumi 186
29. The Wandering Hills 196
30. Forced Landings 203
31. Working Man 207
32. Search Parties 214
33. Voyage along an Ancient Shore 218
34. The Noise of a Crusade 226
35. Desert and Sea 233
36. Winding Down 240
37. Windigog 246

Preface

> Shall we sit here on this Persian rug
> of moss and lichen? The river
> like a knife cuts Precambrian rock
> for us alone, and from its gorge
> ages rise like mists that shawl
> the rounded shoulders of these hills.
> Joanne Hart

I sink into the moss, breathing hard from the short climb. The mists are thinning. Beyond the river's gorge I can see the lake. It moves gently, bright in the morning sun.

When I have rested, I grip a little birch, hoist myself to my feet, turn, and look up. Mountains were here once, tall as the Canadian Rockies. Wind, snow, ice and rain have worn down their peaks to the rounded shoulders of these hills. But the cliff behind me is steep.

One man's lifetime is nothing to Precambrian rock. The face of the stone hasn't eroded any that I can see. Each crevice and toehold is just as it was when I first scrambled up it. I marvel that anything can stay so stolidly the same while the people have so changed.

The few remaining farmers admit that this is no farming

country. They drive school buses or work in the city, and keep cows as a hobby.

The fishermen no longer row out in high-ended dories, ever watchful for a blow from the northwest. They tend the nets in fast motorboats and get weather reports on the radio. 'Tschgumi still drowns men, but not as often as he used to.

The loggers are sober technicians who live at home, commute to work, and, with their brontosaurian machines, cut more timber than whole crews of old-time lumberjacks. They buy bonds and certificates of deposit instead of "blowing it in" on one glorious orgy at the end of the drive.

But the Indians have changed the most. We called them Chippewa, or Ojibway. They spoke of themselves as Anishinabeg, which means the real, original men.

Their language is just right for the northern forest. In a few soft words, conditions of ice, snow, wind, water, and the other forces of vital importance to all life here can be described precisely. I'm not going to use much Anishinabowin in this book, so we won't need a glossary. You'd know, wouldn't you, just from the sound, that "mukwa" is bear and "omeemee" is pigeon? Surely "'Tschgumi" suggests the mystery of the great, cold, spirit-haunted lake.

Maybe you won't believe everything I tell you. That's all right. No hard feelings. I wouldn't swallow some of this stuff either if I hadn't seen it. But credibility should not be the concern of an eyewitness. His job is just to tell what he saw. It's up to other people to make the judgments.

In telling what I saw, I haven't been able to keep all events in the order in which they happened. The chapter about a cave, for instance, starts with childhood memories and ends with a return in later years. When the narrative is pursuing bears or bankers it wanders in time wherever the spoor may lead.

It has been a relief to say some things here that I wouldn't have dared to include in my articles for outdoor magazines. Some hard facts about equipment would have enraged advertisers. Certain of my youthful indiscretions violated the law and the sportsman's code. I'm not proud of these, but they did happen.

This isn't a how-to-do-it book, but I have described a few tricks for living in the woods and on the water, methods that I would like not to be lost. Technique is lighter than equipment and easier to carry over portages. Some of my practices are contrary to the advice of established authorities. I don't mean to assert that those people are wrong. I'm just telling how things went for me. You can take your choice.

More controversial, or anyway more bitterly argued, are the questions of progress versus conservation. Again, I have tried simply to report memories from some battlefields of that never-ending war. But I have been unable to speak as an honest neutral. So I may as well confess that I am one of those radical troublemakers, now being compared to Nazis and Stalinists, who nag at the human race to relax, a little, its strangle-hold on the quivering planet.

My acknowledgments are short because testimony should be given from recall rather than from research. But I thank my wife, my daughter and my son for dredging deep into remembrance of things past.

And now let's look at one of those remote ages that rise out of the mists above the river.

J. L. P.

Chapter 1

THE VIEW FROM THE HILL

>Hit! Hit! McGonagle thinks he's it!
>First he hired me,
>Then he fired me,
>Then he gimme the shit!

The rude carol stirred the soul, as might some military march or pealing national anthem.

I couldn't yet have been expert at walking, but I was swinging my arms and keeping up—and trailing clouds of glory from my last place in the line of small-fry strung out behind the column of marching men. All of us, big and little, were tramping in unison down the dusty street, singing our war-song over and over, a band of brothers, surely irresistible in our righteous resolve. We were ready to take on the railroad or the world.

Only two things were lacking: support and opposition. A few people were standing on the plank sidewalk, calm as mud turtles on a log. The storekeepers watched sadly from their doorways. A slightly more enthusiastic group came out of the saloon, cheered a little, and waved. But by the time that I, the last marcher, had come abreast of them they were already crowding back through the swinging doors, jostling each other in their haste to end the parched interlude.

On the other side of the street, and running far beyond it, stood a tall fence of heavy, vertical steel bars, pointed at the tops, a formidable barrier. Behind it rose the soot-darkened brick car shop, the enemy stronghold.

But no hostile officials glared down at us from its windows. No company detectives were taking photographs or writing down names. No thin, blue line of policemen stood with truncheons ready, barring our way. When we reached the great iron gate in the spiked wall, we found it not only unlocked, but hanging insultingly open.

We paraded back and forth for a while between these symbols of public indifference and corporate nonchalance. The march slowed and stopped. The song died. So soon I met the deadly apathy that lazily reaches out to crush the wing feathers of man's aspirations.

William A. McGonagle, as a young engineer, had laid out the line of the Duluth, Missabe and Iron Range Railroad from the head of Lake Superior, over tamarack swamps and through cuts in the hills, to the iron mines of northern Minnesota. In 1910 he was its president, and something of a father-figure in the village of Proctor. The community depended on him and the DMIR for its livelihood, for the civic and private benefits extended in that age of company paternalism, and for the consistent disregard of small expropriations of supplies, anything from wooden ties to screwdrivers, that were obviously needed worse by the workers than by the Railroad.

Emotion rose strong and proud in me again when I recited the lyric at the supper table that evening. The s-word didn't make a big hit, but the corrections were mild. A family that had been in the banking business for as many generations as ours was conservative in its views. My father, though, was not taking sides against local labor. He reminded me, on a later occasion, that any increase in railroad pay would be good for the town and for the bank.

෬෫෨෬

Another shaft of light breaks through the mists that shawl that hill where I was born. I remember long, dusty days that always ended with the setting sun in my eyes.

My father had acquired a partly tamed monster, a Chalmers. He had conceived the daring enterprise of driving, with my mother and me, to San Francisco where her brother, a naval officer, was stationed. Daring, because nobody had thought of filling stations yet or automobile repair shops. The only road, for much of the way, was the old wagon trail through mud, sand and mountains.

Gasoline was available from time to time at general stores in towns along the railway. These were often far apart, but we carried plenty of cans. Blacksmiths could mend broken parts, and every car owner had to be a reasonably competent mechanic. Breakdowns were frequent, though, and repairs took time.

That was all right with me. I was five years old and excited to be seeing real cowboys and western Indians. I drew pictures of them, from life or fresh memory, while my father bent over the obstinate engine, patched and pumped up a tire, or lay, with feet protruding, under the car.

At one of the stores he bought me what I had been begging for: a lariat. After that, during repair waits, I stalked the horses and cattle that came to stare at us.

Those wild and frowzy creatures never let me get close enough even to attempt to rope one of them. I decided that, these being modern times, I would lasso an automobile.

My father strained beneath the Chalmers. My mother knitted. Unobserved by either of them, I tied one end of the rope to a stout fence post and the other around my waist. I crossed the road and stepped back toward it, dropping the rope in the dust. Then I waited, patient as a spider, for my victim.

He came at last, a young man in a hurry, barreling down the lane at a speed that must have approached fifteen miles an hour.

At the last moment I jumped back. The rope snapped out of the dust, taut across the road. I had him!

But no, he swerved his car. It plunged into and over the ditch, bounced against a boulder and came to rest, right side up.

The driver stood up behind the wheel and swore. A stream of curses, vivid and heartfelt, addressed to my mother and me.

My father crawled out from under the car, black with grease and dirt. He looked around, confused. He didn't know what all the shouting was about, but he knew his duty. In that remote era, a gentleman did not allow such language to be used in the presence of a lady, let alone directed at her. He walked menacingly toward the other driver.

"Hamilton," my mother called, "he saved John's life."

She explained the situation, the guy gradually quieted, and my father helped him get his car back on the road. The enormity of my action was made clear to me. At repair waits after that my mother's eyes were on me rather than on her knitting.

One of those waits was different.

We had been driving all day through hot, dry desert without farms, ranches or even a shanty. We might not have been able to follow the crumbling old ruts left by wagon wheels if we hadn't also been guided by skeletons of animals that had fallen beside the track. My parents' faces were like masks, white with alkali dust. I was crying for water, but it had all been poured into the steaming radiator.

At sunset the Chalmers croaked to a halt in a dry creek bed. My father dug in the sand, but could find no moisture. He took two buckets from the car.

"I'll walk on and come back as soon as I find water."

I lay in the back seat with my head on my mother's lap. It was cool now and I went to sleep. I woke often to ask whether father had gotten back yet with the water, then slept again.

At last there was the squeak and grate of iron-rimmed wheels.

"Whoa."

A lantern came jolting down into our gulley, and a bottle of water was at my lips.

I slept through the wagon ride and woke only when I was carried into the long bunk shack of a sheep ranch. Lanterns were lit. All hands were awake to inspect the strange guests. This was not a tourist age nor a tourist country.

A blanket was stretched across a corner covering the cot that had been assigned to my mother and me. I slept again.

Next morning my father returned to the Chalmers. Then or on some later day, he brought it back to life. We thanked our hosts and drove on, up into foothills.

At Salt Lake City we were joined by Uncle Fred, another brother of my mother's. He had come by train to go through the rest of the mountains with us.

That was good for us. He had become skilled at repairing machinery at the family farm in West Virginia. With two mechanics the repairs went more quickly.

Once a broken part proved too much for the local blacksmith. The question was when a replacement might reach us, if ever. Uncle Fred took the jagged iron in his satchel and boarded the train east.

The days passed. I stared at the trophy heads that stood out from the faded wall paper in our hotel. Finally a train brought the uncle back to us with a shining new part, obtained at the factory.

In San Francisco there were joyous greetings, gallant dinners to eat, and sights to see, including Chinatown. I wanted to go into a theater with the entrance shaped like a dragon's mouth. "Oh no! They might chop you up with hatchets. Those people are dangerous." One of them was, as I will relate in another chapter.

"They are honest, though." Aunt Leonore had a Chinese maid. The navy favored Chinese and Philippino servants. But no Japanese. They were already recognized by our Pacific men of war as the future adversaries.

We took the train east, in luxury now, with the Chalmers in a box car. Things hadn't changed much at home during the months that we had been away. Demonstrations had not gone so far as a strike.

That was to come later. As long as I lived in Proctor the horses continued to enjoy their rest in the street, their heads drooping and tails switching, while long trains of cars, piled high with red ore, drawn and restrained by enormous locomotives fore and aft, clanked at their leisurely pace through the town, over the edge of the hill, and down to the ever-hungry docks.

You can see a far way from that hill. At its foot is the green valley of a river. Your eye follows its shining course into Spirit Lake, so named because it is haunted by the ghosts of a pair of star-crossed lovers. They were Sioux and Anishinabe instead of Montague and Capulet, but the reaction of the elders was the same, and brought the same tragic outcome.

Downstream, the river sweeps on into a bay or estuary, protected from the lake by the world's longest freshwater sandbar, the Point, which curves in an eight-mile arc between Minnesota and Wisconsin. This stretch of dunes and beaches has been important to me, as it must have been to many other people who, down through the centuries, inhabited the hills north of it and the forested plain to the South.

On a calm day my mother would sometimes make a nest of cushions for me in a canoe and paddle down the bay shore to a

desolate area known as the barrens. For cold drinking water we would walk through pines to the lake side. I would wade out and fill a jar, then hurry back with goose pimples on my legs. We would eat our sandwiches and my mother would read to me for a while. Then I'd splash through the pools and shallows of the sheltered bay side snatching at their slippery inhabitants, or sit on a piece of driftwood and draw pictures.

After a few of these excursions my mother let me take a place in the canoe's bow and showed me how to get a paddle in and out of the water without interfering too much with our progress. Soon I was paddling alone in the stern while she sat facing me, giving instructions as needed, until I was able to progress in a reasonably straight line instead of in circles.

When the boating season ended I was taken into the Poirer Brothers shop and fitted with a small pair of smoke-tanned moccasins with a loop sewn in on each side for snowshoe thongs. The place was rich in Indian smells: wood smoke, newly cured furs, spruce pitch, and the sweet grass that Anishinabe women used for the dolls and baskets that were part of the stock in trade.

The Poirers made, right there, whatever you needed for the woods. Each of us had a pair of Poirer snowshoes. The brothers cut and sewed canvas to make a tent to my father's specifications, which he wisely allowed them to modify according to their own judgment.

In winter the tent opened along one side to reflect down the heat from the fire. In summer a matching tent of mosquito netting was tied inside it. When the weather was hot and still you could prop up the canvas walls to catch even the feeblest breeze, without getting bug-bitten. I still have that tent, much patched and many times waterproofed. It is heavier than modern tents, but more versatile: comfortable on a hot July night, or, with a good fire, in tree-cracking cold.

Social activity in the summer season centered on the Point: swimming, canoeing, rowing, sailing. In winter it often took the form of a picnic. Guests would bring their snowshoes. We would walk up the drifted ice and around the waterfalls of one of the streams that run down the steep north shore into the lake. There a fire would be built in the shelter of rocks and overhanging evergreens. After the steaks or sausages there would be good talk and usually some singing. Middle class families of the time accepted and enjoyed this kind of entertainment.

Working people were just as familiar with the woods, or more so. When a man was out of a job there were always the logging camps. He would find heavy work there, and long hours, but the pay was steady and there was plenty to eat. For some it was a career, for others a way to survive hard times, which were more severe than recent recessions, but didn't last so long. Farmers would hire out their horses and themselves for winter work in the camps.

The very rich, too, used and enjoyed the wilderness to a much greater extent than they do today. They would have themselves put

ashore, you might say marooned, on some island or distant bay of Lake Superior. There, while "their Indians" carried up tents, packs, canoes, whiskey, tackle boxes, and patent folding furniture from the beach to the camp site, they would watch the fishboat or tug that had brought them fade into the distance. It would return some weeks later to carry them back to civilization, filled with stories of happy hardships and epic flyrod combats.

During the summers of the early years our family rented a cottage on the Point, and later, with the increasing mobility provided by the automobile, on one of the inland lakes. My brothers and I spent most of the day in the water, coming ashore at evening with bleary, washed-out eyes that saw color rings around the glow of each kerosene lamp.

I assumed that my father must be one of the world's best swimmers. He was the first in our summer colony to learn the "Australian crawl." I swelled like a proud bullfrog as I watched him thrash the calm water with that new and spectacular stroke, imported, it was said, from the south seas. It soon became standard for all free-style racing, and I suppose that today's swimmers could hardly imagine a time when it didn't exist. Unlike the side stroke, which had been, until then, the speediest, it was performed in a face-down position. In those early versions the head was turned up for a quick bite of air every fourth stroke. Its practitioners not only left other swimmers behind but also produced a noble splashing that drew the attention of the parasoled audience.

I was hot to learn the new method but found it difficult, especially that timed breathing. When I had mastered it, and, several years later, beat my father in one of our informal races, we were both delighted. I decided then that I was some swimmer. I had not yet learned how tough the world is nor how many people there are in it who can do anything better than I can.

Chapter 2

HAUNTED CAVERN

> "Have not all races had their first unity from
> a mythology that marries them to rock and hill?"
>
> Yeats

The trip to Gallipolis took a long time. My mother had been a little worried, but she and I slept soundly, safe under the guardianship of a well-tipped porter. We left his car at Chicago and transferred to the obsequious and efficient management of another uniformed black man.

At meal times we made our way through the day coaches. These were hot, unventilated cars whose inmates sat or slept with shoes off and shirts unbuttoned. For tables they placed battered paper suitcases on their knees, spanning the space to the spouse or sibling on the opposite seat. On these they spread sandwiches, oranges, bananas, pop, and crackerjack. Popcorn crunched under foot. I enjoyed the luxurious meal in the dining car, the thrill of the passage back through the subculture, and the feeling of relief when we reached the realm of the porter.

Time and the clicking wheels brought us, at night, to a strange city where we must leave his protection. According to my father's written instructions, we were to take a taxi to the other station. But there were no taxis.

My mother stood on the platform, suitcase in her left hand, my hand in her right. Fear flowed down through that trembling grasp and filled me.

The streets were dark and so were the people. The black men, up to now our guardian angels, took on a threatening aspect. Several of them were eyeing us with an apparent calm that obviously masked evil intentions.

I felt the grip tighten. My mother had made up her mind. She stepped down from the platform and along the street at a fast walk—for me, a run. Into darkest Africa.

The jungle was quiet except for the drumbeats of the tattooed cannibals, a rhythm that I could distinctly feel even though I could not quite hear it.

The onslaught was delayed, but we knew that it would come. Our footsteps clattered, without opposition, through an empty warehouse district. Then the familiar big-city smell of coffee beans and horse manure gave way to the strange, sour reek of tenements.

Suddenly it happened. A huge black man hurtled from a doorway. I heard the thud as my mother staggered against me under the impact. I fell, then clambered up, waiting for further blows.

Our assailant stood tall above us, head and shoulders waving from side to side. He was growling at us, muttering some unintelligible demands.

I caught the words, "Pardon, ma'am."

His knees sagged and he settled gently to the sidewalk, first sitting and then subsiding further until he was flat on his back. His boozy breath poured out in a long and comfortable snore.

My mother grabbed my hand again and we dashed on. I can remember nothing more after that but the panting desperation of running for our lives until we stumbled out into the railroad yards. We found our car there with our berths made up by another bowing and smiling porter.

Later, on the last leg of the journey, there were no Pullmans. Now that we were daycoach passengers ourselves, the others around us seemed less outlandish. My mother chatted with the women, and I made cautious contact with children of my own age.

The thrill of the new experience faded. I drank heavily from the water tap at the end of the car, but paid for that indulgence with frequent trips to the unclean toilet. When the heat and smells became unbearable we opened the window and were met with swirling soot and blasts of pelting cinders, one of which immediately found its way into my eye.

When the window had been closed and the cinder had been removed I was tired and conscious of being profoundly dirty. It was a long time before I heard the conductor chant, "Gallipolis."

※

When my grandfather was in the money, nothing was too good for his family. Aunt Emma came out of art school a fine portraitist. Uncle Jack was at Annapolis, Aunt Daisy at Radcliffe. Uncle Fred was graduating from Harvard and intending to take the medical course. Uncle Sandy was ready to start college.

But their father, like many frontier businessmen, was a high roller. After the panic of 1893 his milling and real estate interests collapsed. He had to admit that Superior was not going to become the Chicago of the North after all. He sold out and put the proceeds into a coal mine at Gray's Flats, West Virginia, a town no longer on the map.

This was a time when the railroads and the big coal operators were combining to choke out small producers by setting prohibitive shipping rates, a form of brotherly cooperation since outlawed. My mother's family assembled at Gray's Flats in 1905 to make her wedding a happy occasion, even though their enterprise was then in the last stages of strangulation.

The family came out of that squeeze free of all assets except one last piece of real estate, Poplar Grove, a farm that specialized in raising tobacco, breeding race horses and losing money. Two of the sons and three of the daughters joined their father there, all determined to restore the family fortunes on the sprawling spread of wooded hills and level river bottom. They did, but only with great effort and personal sacrifice.

※

The aunties were waiting to hug me and then Mother as we stepped down. Beyond them Harry, the coachman, groom and gardener, was holding the horses.

We drove through tree-shaded streets where black, brown and tan people sat watching from porches and where similarly colored children looked up at us from their games in the dust. Then down to the ferry, over the wide river, across the long level of plowed land and up a hill where our iron rims ground over flat stone ledges.

We passed through the grove for which the farm was named. The tall, old trees were a totally different species from Minnesota's sweet-scented but short-lived popples. The house was a plain, square, dignified brick centenarian. Like the trees, it showed its age, but no sign of weakness or decay. Its library smelled of the leather-bound books that lined the walls. There was a billiard room where nobody played billiards any more, and a pianola that gave out music when pumped by foot-power.

There was the big kitchen, where the aunts were already busy. And back of that the double log cabin, with a central chimney opening from a fireplace in each section. Its walls looked as old, true and firm as those of the house. This had been the house-servants' quarters in slavery days.

The field-hands' cabins were in the hollow, that is the valley, below and behind the big house. They were still occupied—by field hands who were white now, and could leave any time they wanted to.

Few wanted to. Their wages were small but, again as in the prewar days, they got free pork, beef, milk, corn and potatoes produced on the Farm. They fed their chickens Farm-grown corn. They dug their own coal out of the ridge beyond. They called me, at six years old, Mistah John. The more change, the more the same thing.

A child from one of the cabins led me up another ridge, farther back in the hills but higher, still overlooking the hollow. Behind great boulders that stood tall like trees, he showed me a crevice in the hillside. I followed him into it.

The narrow entrance opened to a cavern. From inside, someone had dug and ground and hammered a peek-hole through the stone. This opening came out high on the face of the cliff. We lay on our stomachs and looked out over the valley below.

I said, "The people who lived here didn't want to be seen."

My new friend nodded agreement.

"But they wanted to know who was coming up the hollow."

"At night the hants come out here."

I couldn't go along with that, and my face showed it.

"You can laugh about hants if you want to. But I know that they're true."

"Did you ever see one?"

"No, but my Uncle Charlie did. He said so. And he doesn't lie. Do you live in a snow house?"

I assured him that our home in Minnesota was not an igloo. I didn't argue further about the ghost-haunts. Maybe they did come out here at night.

The Negroes, when they had finished the day's work on the fields along the river, must have brought their dogs up here to hunt. On cold nights they probably roasted possum beside a fire that reflected light and heat off the sheltering rocks and back into the cave.

As we left the cave I looked up at the smoke-blackened rock overhead.

"There are a lot of black people in Gallipolis. Why are there none on this side of the river?"

"The Kukluxes run all the nigras out after the war. They never come back."

I came back often, then and in later years.

Before white men or black men farmed here, before the land along the Ohio was cleared, this might have been a hide-out for the pirates that preyed on river traffic and murdered foot-travelers on the Natchez Trace. That's too long ago for anything but a guess. And yet the cave would have been ancient even then.

For centuries, and maybe for millennia, men must have dragged the gutted carcasses of deer up this steep hillside, while women hoed corn in the creek bottom below. And always they had to be ready to take cover at a warning from the lookout.

But even before that, the cave would have stood here behind the boulders waiting for the people. Ever since the river made it. This is an old place.

Chapter 3
LA BELLE RIVIERE

> I am with you, men and women of a generation,
>   or ever so many generations hence . . .
> Just as you are refresh'd by the gladness of the river
>   and the bright flow, I was refresh'd.
> Just as you stand and lean on the rail yet are hurried
>   by the swift current, I stood yet and was hurried.
>   Whitman

The bottom land ended in a fringe of trees. These kept a firm hold on the world, running their foundations way back under the West Virginia cornfields. They needed that grip to hold the line of their outer edge because, on that side, every so often, the river tore the land away. Here the roots came writhing out of the earth like snakes. They grasped driftwood, coiled around planks, chunks, and logs as though to crush them. They slithered down into the masses of brush and weeds that sprouted after one flood, were draped in soft, gray flotsam by the next flood, and were carried away by another.

Several horses stood in the shade, comfortably free of saddles and bridles, but tied to the tree trunks with ropes. Their owners had paid the nickel each for passage instead of the fifteen cents that en-- titled a rider to take his mount across. They would do their city duties on foot and return, before the day was over, with their receipts, prescriptions and purchased goods, to ride back into the hills.

As we left the level cropland, one of the tethered horses whinnied. Our mares looked straight ahead, pretending not to hear. The carriage tilted suddenly forward, lurching as it dropped into the ruts that zigzagged down the bank. My aunts continued chatting while Aunt Ruth reached for the brake, but I hung tight to the steel brace beside my seat.

I wasn't the only one who was nervous. The roan was as placid as the ladies, but the bay, Sweet Marie, arched her neck and stepped high, feeling her hooves slip in the steep mud.

Below us, the paddle wheel was turning just enough to hold the ferry in place beside the moored raft that served as its dock. The engine huffed out a cloud of dark smoke. Several foot passengers and a mule-drawn wagon were already aboard. A whisper-thin man, his face blacker than any Negro's, stood bent, gripping a rope that wound around a stanchion to hold the ferry to the shore. Cap Lane leaned on the rail. He was not rushing us but everybody was ready for the order to cast off.

The Ohio, the beautiful river, swirled past, paying no attention to horses or humans. It swung the dock out a little and poked a brown finger between the ramp and the shore. Sweet Marie and I knew that we were being asked to place ourselves in the hands of an enormous power, inexorable as birth, death or the wind.

At the water's edge Sweetie planted her feet and stood, regardless of clucked orders. Her eyes rolled wildly. She would go no farther.

Aunt Ruth, still talking, not even looking at the mutinous mare, took the whip from its stand and gently lowered its tip to just touch the bay rump. Sweetie flinched as though she had been struck a vicious cut, then hurled her weight forward. The carriage surged into the water. The horses clambered up the planks, tearing the wheels out of the river's muddy grip

"Mornin', Miss Emma. Mornin', Miss Ruth."

"Good morning, Captain Lane."

Already the bar had been slid across the entryway and our wheels chained and blocked. The boat let go its frail hold on the bank. Instantly it was swung sideways and swept downstream.

I looked to the captain for swift, decisive action, some desperate maneuver to save us. Maybe he would lower the lifeboat. Women and children first! But he had put one foot on our carriage hub and was making that amount of conversation required by politeness. The brief discussion of crops and weather was broken once by an order slung sideways to the deck hand. The aunts did not offer to pay fare, nor did he ask it. His dock was tied to our land.

This was the most liberated of free enterprises. Some kind of ferry had been going back and forth here forever, or at least as long as anybody could remember, with no subsidy from either state. The Captain operated this one with the nickels from his regular passengers, quarters from the wagon drivers, and an occasional half-dollar when one of those automobiles dared to grind through the mud and spin-splatter up the ramp.

There were no high-pay industries in these parts to seduce his pilot and his deck hand, and no welfare to lure them into indolence. Nobody had heard of such a thing as a minimum wage. He had to pay them something to keep them alive and working. Not enough to fatten them, though. They wouldn't have expected that. Obesity had never been a problem for the people of these hills. The boat's fodder, big chunks of slatey coal, was personally dug by the three mariners from the ridge above Lanes' Hollow.

The engine huffed and the wheel churned, pushing the bow back upstream, recovering the lost water. I got braver too, put my foot on the little oval step between the wheels, and hopped down to the deck.

The black white man had opened the furnace door and was pushing an iron rod into it. I looked over his shoulder, felt the heat on my face, and breathed in the rich smell of soft coal smoke. I have loved that odor ever since.

The rectangular piece at the end of the rod moved back and forth through the long, deep glare, raking and prodding the flames into greater fury. I was getting a glimpse of the underworld and this was a chief devil. He drew out the rod and loaded in great shovelfulls of slab-sided, sin-blackened souls.

The iron door clanged shut and the hell-show was over. I went up to the bow and stood looking down at the shifting, speeding water, not really scared any more, but still awed by the relentless force that moved beneath us.

We curved in to the Ohio side too far upstream. We were going to ram the shore. But, no, the engine subsided, the current carried us down, and we eased neatly in beside the dock.

This was no muddy, river-torn, farm and mountain landing. Our carriage wheels grated and rattled up a long, firm slant of cobble stones to the green central square of Gallipolis, French Town, the old city on *la Belle Riviere*.

Eventually the Captain was forced out of business by the free bridge that the federal government erected a few miles upstream at Point Pleasant. My family and millions of other passersby were carried by that tall and dignified structure for many years. Then the bridge tired, stumbled, and let go. Automobiles dropped end over end, and people waved arms and legs before they splashed into the Ohio.

◦₃₈◦

Walking over the hills above the farmhouse I asked Aunt Ruth a question that had puzzled me.

"You are good to kids. Why don't you get married and have some of your own?"

"I never found anybody that would have me."

I considered that statement.

"That can't be so. You are nice. And pretty, and a good cook, and such a good rider."

I didn't get a satisfactory explanation then, nor in the years that followed. But as the first of the coming generation of nieces and nephews, I benefited greatly from her single state and from that of her brothers and sisters.

She and Aunt Emma especially devoted their time to me during our visits to Poplar Grove Farm and theirs to Proctor. They read good books to me. They brought me watercolors, crayons, and paper, and Aunt Emma showed me how to use them. I loved to draw or paint while one or the other of them read aloud.

They had me reading to myself at an early age. When I started school at six I had read *Just So Stories*, *The Jungle Books*, *Robin Hood*, *Legends of King Arthur's Court* and Selma Lagerlof's *Adventures of Nils*.

It paid off in first grade. I hated the confinement, and kept my eye on the slow-moving clock, but got all A's on my report card. That winter I was sent to read at a teachers' convention, on display as a proud product.

But pride goeth before a fall. I went to hell in the second grade. That was where I came up against arithmetic. My first B was greeted with groans at home, and I felt disgraced. It wasn't long before my parents and I were well pleased with any grade better than a flunk.

Every autumn, though, in spite of teachers' protests, my mother took me, and later my brothers, for a five to six weeks' visit to Poplar Grove. With equal regularity, I was delightfully free of discipline as far as the aunts were concerned. I can remember putting the serious question to my mother, "Why can't you be nice to me, like Aunt Emma and Aunt Ruth?"

○❧○

As I grew older, the Farm changed. The tobacco barn was no longer draped with graceful, sweet-smelling leaves. A couple of sulkies, light little two-wheeled racing carriages, were stored in it now. They just stood there in their cobwebs. Colgot, the dignified but excitable stallion, was as big as an elephant. He had been imported from Belgium to sire plow horses, not racers.

Saddle horses were still important at Poplar Grove, but now they were quick, strong and wiry like the farm help, and, like them, had learned the knack of handling cattle. Every Sunday I'd be up before daylight to ride with Uncle Sandy back into the hills to check the condition of the pastures and of the white-faced Herefords who were increasing year by year as the hills were cleared.

On weekdays I went alone, following old wagon roads that led back beyond our last gates. Several of these trails still showed regular use and yet, like some Canadian portages that I was to meet later, might lead an inexperienced traveler into difficult or dangerous passages. Some of the rocks over which they passed sloped at such an angle that I would have to dismount. While I watched my own footing I would hear the mare's hooves scraping and scrambling behind me. We would both be scared, but I figured that if other people and other horses had made it, so could we. We always did.

At the point where one of these steep down grades leveled off into a valley floor, I looked up and saw three children watching me.

When they found themselves discovered they dashed to a sagging, weatherbeaten cabin, and dived into a hole in its rock underpinnings, pop, pop, pop, like groundhogs into a burrow.

From preparatory school and college, I came back to Poplar Grove at every spring vacation. I used to run long distances then and plunge into the Ohio, very cold and muddy at that season. I was always in training for something or other, and this provided the excuse for such performances, but of course their main purpose was to show off.

I still have the photo of my fiancee, sitting pretty and incredibly young, in the mouth of the cave. In following years we came back with children. Still later, when all the other aunts and uncles were dead and Aunt Emma, in her nineties, had been taken on a final trip across the river to the hospital, my stiffening knees climbed the slope to the cave one more time.

Maybe men will drag meat into it again some day, and women will hoe in the hollow, while a reliable girl-child watches through the window in the rock for approaching enemies.

It is an old place, but good as new.

Chapter 4

THE CITY AND THE LAKE

"The coldest winter I ever experienced was the summer I spent in Duluth. . . . But it's the only town I know of where a man can spit three blocks."

Mark Twain

We parasites rode in relaxed comfort. Our host appeared to be almost asleep, his fur cap nodding forward over the reins. He would have left his timber farm before daylight, so it was only natural that he should be dozing now, as early winter evening closed in.

His horses trudged stolidly up the hill, indifferent to the wind and to the added drag of several sleds fastened to the sleigh. They were thinking about oats and the fragrance of green, July-cut hay in a log barn that came closer at every step.

I had dashed out near the foot of the hill and slipped my towrope around a brace that supported one of the side boards. Since then I had been sitting on my sled, the end of the rope wrapped around my mittened hand. I was reasonably comfortable, with my head withdrawn, like a turtle's, into the carapace of my mackinaw collar.

Like the turtle I was wary. My head had disappeared but my eyes were peeking out through the collar opening. So I acted swiftly when the dreamy driver erupted. As he snatched the whip from its tube, I opened my hand, allowing the rope to run clear of the brace. By the time his big rubber shoepaks hit the snow my sled was reversed and I was pushing off down hill.

So were the other turtle-leeches. We did not slide far. After a short pursuit the teamster halted and stood cursing us. We slued our sleds to a stop and listened to the heartfelt stream of mixed English and Norwegian. When he was back on his seat and clucking to the horses, we were passing our ropes through his sleigh braces again. It was all standard procedure for a child homeward bound at the end of a winter school day in Duluth.

Mark Twain's comments describe the city. Its streets swing at precipitous angles up and down and crosswise around curving hillsides, cooled by an enormous ice block for half the year and by winds from 'Tschgumi during much of the other half.

When I was six we had moved down the hill from Proctor.

But only part way down. On winter mornings I could plunge belly-bump, prone on my Flexible Flyer, down the long slant of Woodland Avenue, steering the runners through convenient piles of horse manure to brake my speed when the street was too icy. I would slue around a couple of corners, and finally swing broadside, scraping to a stop in the school playground. The mile had taken only minutes.

The bad news was the uphill walk home for lunch and again when school closed in the late afternoon. But we could often mitigate this by hooking a ride. A new driver might react in outraged violence. An old hand would seldom even look back.

The first trucks were even better than teams, taking us home at an early hour. Later models were too fast to catch.

School was open every weekday. It never occurred to us that maybe we should stay home in bad weather. Since we were not dependent on bus transport, a blizzard just meant that we bundled up tighter and started earlier. We had confidence in our friendly teamsters who came to town early and had always opened a fairly good trail by school time.

When a student entered the classroom with the white of frostbite showing on a nose or an ear, the teacher would tell him to rub snow on it. We know now that this was exactly the wrong therapy, but it never seemed to damage anybody much except that the frozen part had to be protected more thoroughly for another time.

School boards seldom dared hire a married woman, however qualified. People would object that she had a husband to look out for her and didn't really need the job. Most of our teachers were gray veterans. These old misses, for some reason that I cannot explain, were consistently kind and conscientious, generous with their help beyond the hours of duty. I remember individual teachers well and look back on them with gratitude, a sentiment that never occurred to me at the time.

Old men, of course, always think that things were better when they were young. Maybe we're right, and that's the way the world keeps on trending. Anyway, it seems to me that people were happier in those first years of the century than they have been since.

In spite of all the hard work and low pay there was an optimism, a heartening confidence in continuing improvement. God was clearly on the job and in good health.

His competitors, Darwin, Marx and finally Freud, were standing by, ready to help Him as needed or to take over the work entirely if He should prove incapable of meeting modern requirements. Education, democracy and science would soon cure any human ills that might prove too difficult for Divine Providence.

The new moving pictures were telling us about drug abuse, but not by decent people like us, only by Mexicans or Asian perverts in darkened dives. The automobile was coming in, thrilling us with windy, dusty speed. It sent unsophisticated country horses into rearing revolt. But it was killing only a few people and had not yet taken over and standardized our lives. The numbing grip of network television was still far in the future. The air and water were clean in the country and not very dirty in town.

A few members of the Grand Army of the Republic still marched in Memorial Day parades, but most of them rode in bunting-draped carriages. Wars, since their big one, had been short, exciting, and usually won quickly by our side. The opponents had been Indians or other men with dark and greasy skins, in tropical countries. The army knew how to handle them. The formula combined words from an old Civil War song with a reference to the new government rifle:

"Underneath our starry flag, civilize 'em with a Krag."

So when Pancho Villa rode over the border and shot up Columbus, New Mexico, American schoolboys were happy. A war at last, when our whole lives had seen nothing but tiresome years of peace. Our soldiers would civilize that bandit in a hurry.

What a sendoff we gave the volunteers, as they marched in their new uniforms, with flags flying and band playing, down to the Northwestern Depot! The departure of other soldiers, a year later, for World War I was nothing like it: just ordinary guys in street clothes, without flags or music, and carrying suitcases. War was old stuff by then, anyway. The Mexican campaign had been a disappointment.

The newspapers had thrilled us repeatedly with detailed reports of how Villa was caught, surrounded, this time for sure, no chance to escape.

He always did. Not many people got killed. A friend of ours was seriously wounded by a Mexican—not bandit, but bug. He sat on a scorpion.

The dark people in the movies were just as malicious and greasy as ever. Somehow, though, they looked less incompetent.

༺༻

Long before my time the citizens of Duluth, eager to beat the rival port of Superior in the race for waterborne commerce, had, in a frenzy of flying sand, shoveled out a passage for the river current through the Point near the Minnesota shore in time to meet a qualifying deadline. The federal government rewarded this effort of municipal patriotism with a proper canal.

That word, canal, may bring to mind some quiet, pastoral water road, overhung by droopy willows, as in Holland or upstate New York. This canal is different. It is guarded on both sides by great concrete piers that run far out into the lake. These stand high above calm water but are washed over by storm waves. After several promenaders were swept over the parapets the Coast Guard erected gates, locked against the public when a northeaster blows.

Above these piers stands a graceful steel structure known as the aerial bridge. It was built high to allow the passage of tall sailing ships, and strong to resist the fury of the lake. It has been doing that now for a hundred and twenty years, so you must respect it as well as admire it. But it has been the scene of a number of fatal accidents.

Down from its height hung a car, a moving platform with gates at each end and cabins along the sides where the passengers could take shelter from the lake winds. The open space in the center held wagons and carriages, except on regatta days, when the whole ship was filled with masses of shouting, pennant-waving humanity. Duluth Boat Club crews could hold their own with the best in the country, and citizens responded as Americans always have to winners.

A voyage on the trans-canal ship was almost as exciting as watching the boat races. Ship, I suppose, is hardly the right word, but what would you call it? When I looked down through its gratings at the waves far below, it seemed more like a balloon or one of those new flying machines.

The life preservers, nautical rings that hung on the ends of each cabin, always stirred my imagination. I used to picture their use in all kinds of desperate emergencies. I earnestly hoped that I would be on board when they were needed.

But I missed it. I wasn't there when a beginning driver forgot the instructions on how to stop his shiny new automobile and clamped his foot down on the accelerator instead of the brake. He rammed a heavily-loaded wagon with its team and driver through the gate, then remembered the correct procedure in time to stop his car on the brink.

The horses sank, pulled down by the weight of the wagon. The driver, a non-swimmer, went down too, was carried toward the lake by the current, came to the surface, and sank again. Someone finally remembered to throw in the life preservers. They floated far behind him, like funeral wreaths after a burial at sea.

Jim Ten Eyk, world-famous oarsman and coach of the Boat Club crews, happened to be on the bridge car at the time. He threw off his coat and ran along the pier until he caught up with the struggling figure, still visible occasionally in its swift journey through the canal.

Ten Eyk took time to untie his shoes and kick them off, then ran down the wall again, dived in, and came up behind the man's back.

He clamped an arm across his chest and held him up, foiling his earnest efforts to get a grip on the rescuer and drown them both.

In this one-sided embrace they were swept through the canal, past the lighthouse at its outer end, and out into the lake. Neither Ten Eyk nor anybody else could have held on long in that cold water. But a rowboat had been launched from the Point and arrived in time to take them from the lake and back to safety.

From the vantage point of later years, this accident seems freighted with the symbolism of things to come: man and beast cast into the depths by the triumphant machine.

The traveling car has been replaced by a span, a section of bridge that lifts to let the ore and grain boats through. This speeds auto traffic, but how dull the passage has become! Just another bridge crossing instead of a swaying aerial voyage.

Chapter 5

CHINK

> For ways that are dark and for tricks that are vain,
> The heathen Chinee is peculiar.
>
> Bret Harte

"Fight! Fight! Fight!"

The cry rang out, joyful with the innocent ferocity of childhood and the delight of an unexpected reprieve from the school day's boredom. The landscape was a swelling flurry of scholars, every one of them rushing toward us. A thickening, tightening circle closed around us, shouting, taunting, pushing us together.

When I lived in Proctor, my playmates and I used ethnic terms freely. The Slavic immigrants who lived in the valley below us were hunkies. A marshy stream ran through Frogtown, but that name was derived from its French population, not its amphibian. Polack, dago and nigger were not meant by us as expressions of contempt. They just happened to be the words for those people.

Twice each year a bearded man swung a clear-ringing cowbell as he drove a wagon down the street. Children sent out to sell him rags and bottles addressed him respectfully as Mr. Sheenie. That title aroused no visible resentment and certainly was never allowed to interfere with business transactions.

So when our family moved down to Duluth, I was unprepared for irascible and unforgiving urban reactions.

Everybody but the teacher called him Chink, and he didn't object to that from his old classmates. But when I, the new boy, so addressed him on the playground, his slanted eyes narrowed, his lower lip curled, and he sidled toward me with obviously deadly intentions.

"What do you mean, Chink?"

I stared at him, silent, not understanding.

"My name is Arthur."

"But all the guys call you Chink."

"What my friends call me is none of your business. Because you're not one of them. You big slob!"

I backed away. His cheering section was pouring on courage.

"Hit him, Chinky! Hit the big guy!"

He stepped forward.

Although only a week in the school, I suddenly found that I had friends too.

"Hit him, Peyton! What're you backing away for? Are you a-scared of that little Chinaman?"

A truthful answer would have been "Yes, yes, of course yes. Though he be little he be fierce, and I'm terrified of him." But a second grader wouldn't have said anything like that. Not in those days.

There was no way to avoid battle with honor, or even without it. Now, at the last minute, he was holding back too, but the audience was tightening its circle around us.

A shove from behind slung me against him. Suddenly the air was full of his fists.

I knew nothing of boxing, had no idea of how to ward off the blows that came driving up. He must have had to jump to reach my face, but he got to it all right, and my head buzzed with the shock.

In pain and terror, rather than joy of battle, I hit back as hard as I could. He was no more skilled in the manly art than I. Blood ran down over his mouth and chin. Its source was his nose, but he looked as though he had chewed it out of me.

Desperate minutes passed. Dusty, mindless, bruising minutes. Finally the punches began to slow.

At last we stood gasping, staring wildly at each other. I leaned back, bracing my feet against strong forward pressure. My friends slacked off, muttering their disappointment. I felt for buttons to close my shirt, but they had been torn away.

My adversary wiped a hand across his face and looked down woefully at the red palm. Suddenly he held it out and stepped forward.

For a moment I hesitated, watching him warily. Then I grasped the bloody hand.

"We're friends now, Arthur?"

"That's right. But call me Chink."

CR&O

The treaty thus concluded was soon to be ratified in further action.

The pride of the Endion school had always been the recessional. At the end of each day, a musically talented teacher played a martial air on the piano while the student body marched out of the turreted old building, down alternate flights of steps and stretches of slanting walkway across the hillside yard to the sidewalk. That had been the procedure for as long as anyone could remember.

An opposite but equally ancient custom had been observed annually at the last exit before Christmas vacation. On that happy day the departing students broke the well-drilled ranks and ran across the snow uttering defiant shrieks. It had always been taken for granted that this offense would be forgiven in the goodwill-to-men season, or else forgotten in the vast expanse of the two-week holiday.

A new principal, a woman of iron will, decided to correct this seasonal violation of discipline. The menacing announcement was read in each class that on this last school day of the year the march would proceed in perfect formation to the street level. A group of hulking old males from the eighth grade were deputized to stand along both sides of the parade route and enforce the marching order.

Grumblings were loud and mutinous as the column formed up. We all knew that an invasion of our immemorial rights was taking place. I was certain that somebody else would run, and I was tensed to follow.

Out the door, down the steps and across the walks the rigid procession continued. Miss Thompson's storm troopers, grinning with the pride of new authority, moved back and forth along the line of march, alert for any sign of rebellion. Vile, calm, dishonorable submission!

Some demon, or some angel of martyrdom, took possession of me. I shoved the nearest marcher aside and sprinted for the street, the myrmidons at my heels and the student body in full cry behind them.

I thought that if I could make it to the sidewalk and off the school yard I would be safe. There the Endion constabulary would surely have to leave the pursuit of criminals to the city police.

But those long-legged monsters paid no more attention to property lines than do dogs after a rabbit. Right behind me I heard them pounding, over the public street and across a vacant lot, gaining at every step. They finally brought me down with a skid and a thump in a flying spray of snow.

I fought with the desperation of utter terror. What hideous punishment awaited me in the principal's office I did not try to imagine.

One of the ruffians had me by the shoulders and another was grabbing at my wildly kicking feet. I saw Chink pick up a handful of snow. His hands were packing it while he bent forward, shifting his position, watching for an opening. Then my legs were secured and I was carried, tossing and squirming, back toward the school.

Suddenly a pale and beautiful flower blossomed on the red face of the man at my feet. I can see him yet, wide-eyed through the splattered whiteness, his open mouth filled with snow.

Another missile struck, and then a flight of them, hard-packed, icy, and accurately aimed. My captors dropped me and fell back, shielding their faces. "You're going to get it," one of them shouted at me from under his covering arm. "You're going to get it when you come back to school!"

And so I did, but only a routine scolding and one short afterhours imprisonment. Miss Thompson was not such an ogress after all. At the end of that school year the daily recessional was abandoned.

From that Christmas on, Chink and I were best friends. Our classmates called us Mutt and Jeff after the long and short cartoon characters of the day. Soon we were fishing, hunting, and camping together.

Our early trips were made on foot, out through the suburbs

and over a maze of logging trails through the cutover but resurgent forest. Sooner or later water would gleam through the trees ahead and we would come out on a river or some roadless, cabinless lake. There were trout in the streams, small fish, but very good fried. In the ponds and lakes we hooked out flat round sunfish that had to be eaten carefully on account of the bones. And quite often a long, slimy, fierce-looking pike.

We would climb out on fallen timbers to get our bait into promising water, or wade over gravel bottoms, feeling with cautious feet for the occasional sinkhole. In autumn we would wriggle through tall swamp grass to ambush a coot or walk quietly down an old trail at evening. Sometimes as we came around a curve, there would be a partridge, strutting or dusting or just standing and watching us with long-stretched neck.

The winters that followed were good times for Chink and me. On weekends my father drove us out as far as the road was plowed, and from there we continued on snowshoes to the family cottage at Caribou Lake. This was a flimsy structure, cheaply built for the summer season. At the first good blizzard a ridge of snow drifted in through a crack in the wall, and thereafter held its own in one corner of the living room, growing with each storm until spring. But plenty of firewood was at hand, and even in the coldest weather there was always a comfort zone around the red-hot stove.

Fishing and hunting did not allow us much daylight time in that pleasant area. We crouched on the lake with our backs to the wind, watching for one of our sticks to flip up and signal a deal with a scaly customer below. Back in the swamps the snowshoe hares

were big, white, and swift. They were hard to hit on the run, but if I whistled at one he might brake to a sudden stop and sit there while I took aim. We usually carried a proud bundle of them when we returned to the Sunday afternoon rendezvous at the road's end.

Kids were beginning to take an interest in automobiles. If there were any such things as driver's licenses or driving age limits we hadn't heard about them. My younger brother, Newton, who is mechanically inclined, was driving while he still had to sit on the edge of the seat to reach the pedals.

I have always been backward in motor matters and didn't learn to drive until I was almost thirteen. Then a new world opened. Chink and I could go west to the rich swamps around the sources of the Mississippi, and north to the evergreen forest.

Chapter 6

INDIANS

"The Indians, whose chief Sagamores are well known unto some of our Captives to have been horrid Sorcerors, and hellish Conjurors and such as conversed with Daemons...."

Cotton Mather

Cold gray river reflected cold gray sky. Sheets of rain, lashing in from the Northeast, forced entry at my collar and sleeves. I shifted my grip on the paddle, trying to find unblistered spots on palms and fingers. Then I just sat, a shivering, sodden, dejected lump.

"We stop soon," said Moosh from the stern. "You paddle now and keep warm."

This seemed a sad beginning for an adventure that I had anticipated with such excitement: my first voyage into the great forest of the Canadian shield.

A party of professional men, friends of my family, had invited me, a ten-year-old, to come on their annual fishing trip. They had assigned me to the canoe of a one-eyed old man, whom they spoke of, for reasons not at first evident to me, as "our best Indian."

When I did start paddling again Moosh must have seen that I would not be able to keep it up for long. There was still plenty of daylight left as we came abreast of a little bay, a niche in the river wall But he swung the canoe toward it and called back: "We camp here, yes?"

It was put, with full deference to the white man's authority, in the form of a question. Actually it was an announcement, and a welcome one to his employers. Their approval was prompt. The surgeon, the judge, and the mining engineer were, I suppose, as cold and wet and tired as I was.

While Moosh held the canoe, I stepped stiffly out of it, slipped on the wet rock, and would have splashed into the river if he had not caught me.

Walking cautiously, I carried up the smaller items and set them down on soaked moss because there was no place else to put them. The dripping spruce and jackpine broke the force of the wind but cast a gloomy shadow and did not diminish the drizzle.

One of the Indians had axed open a pine stump to get at its dry interior. Another brought bark from a birch and knelt beside the little bundle, while his partner shielded it from the rain. A flame glowed, throwing warm light on fresh-cut forked poles that were being used to lift the tent, tied to a stout birch ridgepole, into position. A flap running along one side of it was extended to protect the infant fire from the rain.

Soon I heard the happy song of bacon in the pan and smelled baking bannock. Moosh came out of the woods dragging a load of balsam boughs hooked around an axe handle. There were no air mattresses in those days, but when he had stuck the bushy twigs into position and spread a piece of canvas over them the padding was as comfortable. And no modern blowbed smells that good. Quickly I became warm, dry, fed and at ease.

On a steep portage, Moosh could carry as much weight as any of the younger Indians. He was a surprisingly good marksman, too, for a man who had lost his master shooting eye. In those easy times and remote places nobody bothered much about game laws. When camp meat was needed, he would take the little .22 rifle that was our only weapon, leave us for a while in the evening, and come back with ducks or partridge, and sometimes a young doe, shot with lethal precision through the heart or between the eyes.

During school years, the innocence of my Proctor childhood

had been roughly handled. History books set off Indian savagery against the courage and righteousness of the European conquerors. The Indian was a standard villain in the movies, repeatedly defeated in his treacherous attacks on settlers, soldiers or cowboys. When the wild west show had pitched its tents on the circus grounds, I myself had seen real Indians ride down, whooping and shooting, upon a peaceful wagon train. The cavalry got there just in time to prevent a massacre.

I knew that it was only a show, but those Indians were magnificent riders, mean-looking, and genuine. Buffalo Bill had recruited horsemen from the plains, including several veterans of the Little Big Horn. I thought that if they'd been really trying they would probably have wiped out both emigrants and cavalry.

Custer's last stand was vivid in the nation's memory. I had seen that, too, pictured in all its bloody detail, in saloon windows. And there were still many farmers in Minnesota who, as children in 1862, had been tossed from side to side in bumping, swaying wagons and heard their fathers' curses and wildly slashing whips. The horses were pulling their lives out in the desperate effort to escape Indians. That Sioux uprising had brought death to more settlers than any other Indian war. The fear and hatred that resulted had been conveyed, by words or otherwise, to our generation.

So it was comforting to put Buffalo Bill's lean horsemen out of my mind and go back to the movies, where plump warriors, stained dark but with bland white-man faces, kept riding around a circle of wagons while being picked off, one after another, by whiskered marksmen.

My classmates told hilarious stories of the inadequacies of local Indians in their attempts to cope with city life. I had heard the maxim stated, convincingly loud and strong, "Anything an Injun can do, a white man can do better."

Now, dozing off in the warm firelight, I could imagine the kind of camp that my hosts and I would have made in that waterlogged wilderness and how long it would have taken us to make it.

My opinions were further revised in the weeks that followed. I had done enough fishing, camping and canoeing to appreciate the performance of the Indian experts: the silent efficiency of their portaging, the short, quick, unrelenting paddle stroke that daily drove us over seemingly impossible map mileages. In the quiet evening, if I could cast my spoon-bait right to the spot that Moosh pointed out to me, the water would usually swirl around it and I would feel, through line and rod, the life-and-death violence of the under-water world.

༺ ༻

Another invitation brought me as a guest to a logging camp in what used to be called Indian country. One of the loggers, part Ojibway, took me several times to visit his relatives.

The grown-ups welcomed me. I knew that they preferred to talk in Anishinabemowin, but they spoke English well enough, and almost always used it when I was present.

It was different with their boy. He was about my age, but thinner with big, dark, deep-set eyes. I seldom heard him say anything in either language.

At the insistence of his parents, he once took me duck hunting. His battered single shot .410 was held together with haywire. It looked to me about the right weapon for shooting sitting snipe.

I might have been a little gun-proud at the time. An older cousin had given me a double-barreled 16-gauge shotgun, much used, but good. Its choke, the constriction at the end of the barrels that steers the flying pellets in a compact group, had been sawed off. Thus it was not for long distance shooting. It was a forgiving gun, though, that spread the shot over a wide section of nearby landscape. It might miss birds that should have been hit, but, as its donor pointed out, I probably would have missed them anyway. On the other hand, its wide-flung pattern would surprisingly often bring down some unfortunate flyer that should have been missed. It had a way of making up for the too hasty shooting of an excited kid.

The Indian boy walked ahead through bare hardwoods and out into the open, following a trail that softened and dampened underfoot until it became a waterway, a channel through the swamp. Two homemade wooden boats, each equipped with a forked pole and a lard bucket, were pulled up in the grass beside it. A gesture offered me my choice.

I took the one with the least water in the bottom. It still needed some bucket work. When I had it bailed out enough to suit me, my companion was no longer my companion, but a small and distant figure, just visible in the early light, as he poled his boat across the marsh.

I got off a good many shots that day and actually brought down one duck, my first mallard drake. He was big and beautiful, with a green head and with blue chevrons on his wings. I was well pleased with myself when I carried the fat bird back to my hosts' cabin, and they said nothing to reduce my pride. But when their boy came in, he had a gunny sack full.

Something puzzled me about these people. They didn't seem particularly gifted at dealing with the problems and temptations of civilization, nor with gathering its rewards. They were good in the woods, though.

Slowly I came to understand their code of behavior, based on cooperation rather than competition. It didn't work very well in a capitalist society. It was exactly right for the boreal forest.

There were no courts there, no police, no schools. People had to behave responsibly without reward or punishment. It was unusual for anybody to shirk work, throw a tantrum, or steal food. I suppose that the famines of centuries had bred those weaknesses out of them.

This code of behavior, along with the history and traditions of the people, was handed down in the form of ancestral stories that were also parables.

I came back to the logging camp in hunting and fishing seasons and called on my Anishinabe friends. The passing years had not made their son talkative, but at their cabin I met an old lady who was.

Italo Calvino speaks of himself as a link in the anonymous chain without end, by which folk tales are handed down. This nookomis, grandmother, was another such link.

She would not draw up the bucket from the well of the past until the last duck had left the freezing waterways.

"If you tell the old stories while the rivers are open you will sleep with a toad. Come to my house in the winter."

So I walked, one evening, under snow-heavy spruce down the trail to her shanty. It was made of poles and covered with tarpaper. The table was too rickety for my offering of bacon, potatoes and coffee so I set it on the floor. Drafts whistled through the walls and made me turn up the collar of my mackinaw, but they had no effect on the smoky atmosphere or the strangely assorted smells.

Several others came in, children and grown-ups, all Indians. The old lady was illiterate but trilingual. She spoke fluent French, English and Anishinabemowin. For my benefit she kept mostly to English but would sometimes, searching for just the right word, dip into one of the other languages.

When she paused in her recital the listeners would express their appreciation with little sighing cries: eu-eu. This was a quiet applause, not loud enough to interfere with the telling, but I could see that it pleased Grandma.

Some of her stories were classics that I would recognize, years later, in the recordings of anthropologists taken in different parts of the United States and Canada. Others I never met again.

She spoke of sex, excrement and violent death in a manner unheard of in white society of those days. There were no dirty words in Anishinabowin. I could feel a dignity, a religious significance in her stories, through which the wisdom and bitter humor of the ancestors were being carried to new generations.

Mather would have called them conversations with Daemons. Either way, they were good stories.

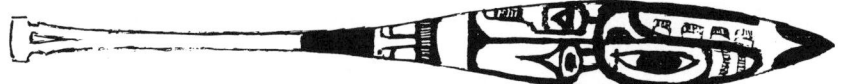

Chapter 7

THIRD RIVER

The wild gander leads his flock through the cool night,
Ya-honk he says, and it sounds to me like an invitation.
                                                                Whitman

There was no place to camp on the shore. There was not even a shore.
    The channel had wandered away from firm ground, through grassy hillocks, cattails, and mottled mounds of water lily roots. Now, in the dying sunset, it brought us into a broad and widening marsh. On both sides, the forest wall had drawn far back from the water, leaving miles of half-drowned bog impassable by boat or on foot.
    Chink and I had spotted Third River's position on the map where it entered the north shore of Lake Winnebigoshish on the pathway of southbound waterfowl. In those days it was a silent stream, whose marshy shores were visited only by a few devotees willing either to take certain risks or to make substantial sacrifices.
    We first approached it over an old logging road, passable, in dry weather, by our high-wheeled little car. When this trail ended at

flowing water, we guessed, correctly, that we had found the right river. We had no idea how far we might be from the lake. We had taken the chance, and now we were stuck with the results.

Not that we were so displeased with those results. We could have turned back at any time as long as a little light remained. But streams of ducks and geese were flowing through the sky above us, out of range, heading for the bay. Under their inspiration we paddled on.

Not for long. We slowed, feeling, in the fading light, for the folded passageway of the channel. When we could no longer follow this we came to a stop. The chill of the autumn night reminded us that we would have to do the best we could with what we had and where we were.

We paddled over the reflected sky and pushed the bow into deepening darkness along its edge until we could move no farther. Chink put his boot over the side, lifted his weight a little on the marsh surface, a sagging old layer of matted grass and rushes. He broke through, and pulled back, dripping black slime into the boat.

"It won't hold us up. Maybe we could put the dog on it."

We laid the sacks of cedar decoys on what little support we could find, spread the tent over them, and pressured the retriever over the gunwale and out on this island. We cut swamp grass and piled it on the boat's bottom. Somehow we found room to squeeze down into the hull on our sides in a horizontal position. It wasn't such a bad night. We even slept a little.

In the morning we went on, a long way, but not to the lake. Time ran out on our day-and-a-half weekend and we turned back. We had been defeated. We had plans, though, for a different approach.

I was working at the Proctor bank during summer vacations. Each Saturday morning was dedicated to the speediest possible getaway after the one o'clock closing. I would put my head down so as not to catch the eye of an approaching depositor, hoping that he would take his hoard to some other teller. Between unavoidable transactions I kept on counting, recounting, and bundling cash, and stamping and stacking debits and credits.

At one o'clock I would be standing beside the door. A customer remarked to my father that if he came in half a second later he was in danger of getting his nose caught in the slam. By one-thirty on most Saturdays, with only rarely a distressing exception, my cash, checks and deposits would be in balance and we would be on our way in my mother's Model T Ford. She never seemed to need it on weekends.

There were no car-top carriers then. We bound the boat to the side of the automobile with long straps fastened together. Some of these ran through the windows, passing over the roof or under the car. These ruled out opening the doors, but it was no trouble to go in and out through the windows.

◦3∞

Winnebigoshish was born when an ice cube melted. That was a big ice cube: seven miles wide and twelve miles long, pressed into the sand by a glacier. It left a shallow lake, less than twenty feet deep in most places, and, for that reason, subject to sudden, violent tantrums when provoked by wind. The road only kissed its shore where the Mississippi flowed out of it to the Southeast.

At high school age many of us have an irrational confidence in our ability to live forever. Death is for old people, a silly boogy man in a mask as far as we young men are concerned.

Chink and I were at that stage of bold ignorance when we made our second try for the river mouth. Otherwise, we wouldn't have crossed Big Winnie, from road to river, in our duck boat. This was a shallow little craft, the color of pale mud, with low, pointed ends, made for sneaking through wild rice or rushes and for hiding in them. It was not designed for carrying cargo. We had left the dog at home, but when we loaded in guns, shells, decoys, camping gear, and ourselves, there were very few wooden inches left above the water.

As I paddled, a little wave licked at my fingers. "That water is cold, Chink, and it's a long way across. Maybe we should turn back. It isn't as though you could swim."

"Since you're such a great swimmer, you can swim back. I'm going to Third River."

The breeze was gentle but occasionally lapped a cupful over the combing. Just a friendly warning. I looked at the sky and saw no threat there. So it went, through the rest of the day.

It took us that long to make the crossing with our overloaded and obstinate little boat. Any time we tried to get some speed up it dipped its nose like a submarine about to dive. I felt very good as we approached the far shore.

We landed at evening on a strange beach where the clean shells of billions of long-dead snails crackled under our boots. This was at the base of a point that led out to an island in the river mouth. We walked across a broad stretch of sand and camped under pines and hardwoods.

A blessed teachers' conference had given us a three-day vacation. At dawn we had glorious shooting from the island and, later in the day, in the rice beds beyond it.

On the second afternoon Chink called to me and pointed out something coming, way down the beach. As we watched, it grew into a pickup truck. Its occupants told us about a different route to this happy hunting ground.

We had to go back the same way that we had come. Our luck held, but I was resolved not to chance that crossing another time. We would drive to the bay the same way those other guys got there. Instead of taking the risks, we would make the sacrifices.

The first of these was a tribute of fifty cents payable to a robber baron through whose homestead the two ruts of the trail ran. I wonder when he slept. He came out of his shanty whenever a car approached at any hour of the day or night. As long as you were speaking English and not Finnish, you could say whatever you pleased about his greed. But there was no use haggling. You paid the full half dollar or you did not pass.

From there on we followed the depreciating trace through its many rough and winding miles, bumping and spinning the tires up each sandy hill, then bouncing down the other side as we gathered speed for the water hole that usually lay at the bottom.

We splashed triumphantly through five of these hazards. The grasping ooze of the sixth laid hold on us, bringing on a swaying, slewing slowdown.

Chink was out of the window and behind the car, pushing with his strong little legs, paying no attention to the mud that the snarling wheels spat over him. These finally found bottom and, with his help, carried us through.

But the next hole was deeper. The car sank until its underpinnings were buried and all forward motion ended.

We cut a stout hardwood sapling, leaving a wedge-shaped end, which we shoved in under the nearly-submerged axle and above a log fulcrum. My position as heavy was bent over the far end of this lever, my toes just touching the ground or sometimes lifted off it, while Chink pushed and pounded rocks in under the raised tire. Then we built a strip of rock pavement running out ahead of it to dry land. Darkness came down, but the sky gave us light enough to finish the work.

There were several miles of beach to get over. We took this at full speed because any slowing down would dig the spinning wheels into a sand trap as bad as the mud.

When the river mouth gleamed through the darkness on our right, we swung up the bank where firm earth permitted stopping and turning. We strung our tent between two big maples, propped its ropes with forked poles, lifted the flap, and built a close-in fire. As I dropped off to sleep I heard the quacking of mallard hens in the rushes.

Chapter 8

FRIENDS

> "I pray God to protect me from my friends.
> I can take care of my enemies myself."
> de Villars

In the wilderness, no matter how egalitarian your philosophy, you learn quickly to be exclusive about the company you keep. The wrong person can make you uncomfortable, unhappy, or dead.

After high school I went east to preparatory school and then to college. Chink went to work but saved his vacation days for the last part of September. My classes started at the end of that month, so we still had almost two weeks together in the autumn woods each year.

I looked around for suitable company at other seasons and learned that it was not easily found or kept. Many a beautiful friendship that bloomed on city pavements or suburban lawns has withered under the greenwood tree. Heat, cold, mosquitoes, cuts, burns, bruises, blisters, persistent rain, smoke that follows you willfully wherever you move around the fire, high, mountainous portages, low, boggy portages, and long hours of paddling against the wind are all common in the northern summer.

These little torments are not so bad when you learn to mitigate some of them and to put up with the others. The Anishinanbeg joked about them and so did Chink. But the next candidate found them outrageous: "Do I really have to endure two weeks of this misery?"

Others became hopelessly demoralized. Unsuspected deficiencies appeared. A friendly fellow became quarrelsome. A good worker turned lazy. He relaxed while I did the chores. The swirls from his paddle didn't eddy back in those deep, firm little whirlpools that follow an honest stroke. I made suggestions. There was no improvement. I shut up and did the work myself.

Another had promised his mother not to go out in the canoe when it was windy. All my arguments failed to shake his filial obedience. We sat out two days of strong tailwind that would have sped us on our way. One afternoon, when we did get caught by a sudden squall, he froze in panic, unable to move his paddle. He insisted on walking around even the easy rapids. I ran them alone while he walked. I waited for him with growing impatience at the lower end of each portage.

Back in town we'd usually remain friends, but often the resolve would be firm in my mind not to get stuck with that guy in the woods again. Conversely, one of my guests politely told me that he had very much enjoyed the trip but that he would never go on another one with me.

Another good friend and I came to a standstill, our canoe adrift, as we first casually, then earnestly, and finally heatedly, debated which course to follow. I felt that this was important. I didn't want to waste miles and hours going the wrong way. He was equally determined. Voices grew loud. A common, if highly improper, epithet was spoken, then resented with exaggerated fervor. We agreed to go ashore and settle the matter. At least we didn't crawl across the packs to get at each other out there on the water.

During the middle ages, trial by combat was probably quite effective in bringing out the truth between contending claims. Providence would surely not allow the false to defeat the true. The lady was clearly virtuous or clearly otherwise, depending on which knight unhorsed the other.

So I feel certain that, if we had gone through with the test, the other man, with God on his side, would have given me a good licking. Then we would have turned in the right direction to the portage we were seeking.

We were on a big lake with a long paddle to shore. We both cooled off before we got there. He must have been more of a gentleman than I, besides having a better sense of direction. We went my way. This took us off the route we had planned and up a beautiful little river where he got close-up photos, and I sketches, of amazingly nonchalant moose feeding on water plants. Eventually we came out on a chain of walleye lakes that we would never have fished otherwise. Who knows what is good fortune?

He was a good camping partner, and I found others: Macdonald, Macrae, and McKenzie. I'm not sure that the consistency of those names is entirely a matter of chance. The Scots have always been good in the Canadian bush. These also got along with me, which was probably a greater accomplishment.

Chapter 9

CRIME AND PUNISHMENT

> I have great comfort in this fellow; methinks he hath no drowning mark upon him; his complexion is perfect gallows.
>
> Shakespeare

An early storm had laid down a carpet of snow three days before the deer season opened. I was following, with the worst of intentions, a neat line of pointed hoof prints. They led me up a ridge covered with birches. At the top I looked back and caught a movement between the white trunks behind me. As I watched it became a man following my tracks. There was the glint of a badge. At that moment he looked up and our eyes met. I took off down the opposite slope.

The snow was not really deep, but I felt as though I were floundering slowly through it, breaking a wide open trail for the game warden. He was coming fast, for a big guy. I could see that I was not going to keep the lead in this race for long.

In the valley below I ran across a half-frozen river. I felt the ice dip beneath me and heard it crack as water surged around my feet. I splashed on not quite breaking through, and grunted up to the edge of the timber. Without stopping I took a quick look over my shoulder. My heavier pursuer was stamping in frustration on the far bank.

As a boy and as a young man I felt that I had a right to take what I wanted from nature when and wherever I could get it. Buying a license for hunting or fishing was as unheard of as for driving. Game laws were themselves a game to be played against the wardens—a spirited, hard-played game that we usually won, with satisfaction, but sometimes lost, with no hard feelings.

The punishment, other than the humiliation of being caught, was nothing very terrible. Chink and I, taken literally red-handed, were given a loud scolding and then chased away. We were kids then, but adult poachers, except big-time killers from the cities, generally got off with small fines.

As the years passed, regulation, enforcement, and penalties became more severe.

⋘⋙

Roe McKenzie and I had just come down a portage into Pickerel Lake at the top of Quetico Provincial Park. A fine, strong wind was blowing from the West. We cut a forked birch for a mast and tied the tent to a crosspiece for a sail. Roe hung on to the corners while I steered. This calls for caution because a canoe without sideboards is not much of a boat for sailing and may be suddenly swamped if the man holding the canvas fails to ease it as needed.

Not this time. We raced the waves down thirty miles of lake and camped near its eastern end, dining well on its round-bodied, golden namesake. (North of the border, pickerel means walleye pike.)

Starting on, next morning, we trailed a spoon bait for more of the same. As usual we had neglected to acquire certain documents such as an Ontario fishing license and a Quetico travel permit. It is a measure of the informality of the times that we didn't trouble to wind in our hand line even as we passed the park headquarters.

A launch came speeding out, manned by a pair of those Canadian types with broad-brimmed hats and underslung jaws. The head man wasn't wearing red, but he still looked as though he might have modeled for the calendar pictures.

"Good morning. May I see your travel permit, please."
"We don't have any."
"Your fishing licenses then."
"We don't have those either."
"I'm sorry, but you'll have to come with us."

We sat in their shore office, looking as young and innocent as we could, while they discussed a procedural problem. To take us to a magistrate at Fort William would be an all-day trip. Such firm enforcement of restrictions on forest travel was something new. Doing a little fishing on the wrong side of the line didn't seem that big of a deal to us, and maybe not to them either. What was more important, this was the dry season.

"I'd hate for you to be down at the Fort if I'd see smoke here."

The chief swiveled from his subordinate to us.

"I tell you what we'll do. The permit fee is $2.00. That lets you fish inside the park. You just pay that and I'll write one out for you. That stretches the rules a bit, but then . . . ."

That would have been fine with us if we had had $2.00. I did have a checking account in Proctor, but no checkbook with me. Cash and checks were not equipment that we had expected to need on this trip.

If they would give me one of their own checks I'd change the name of the bank. They had no checks. Again, the glum impasse.

I saw a brown paper bag on the shelf. "I'll write you a check on a piece of that bag." They weren't so sure about that kind of financing, and besides there was nothing else to hold the sugar.

"All I'd need would be a little piece from the edge."

Nobody said anything, so I tore it off without spilling much sugar, borrowed their pencil, wrote the order, and handed it to the chief. He studied it for a few moments, then put it into a drawer and filled out the permit. The transaction completed, they invited us to stay for lunch.

In the course of time the sticky-sweet little brown check cleared and was paid, not without comment from my coworkers at the bank.

Warning to brother poachers: don't count on that kind of treatment if you get caught fishing without a license in Ontario nowadays.

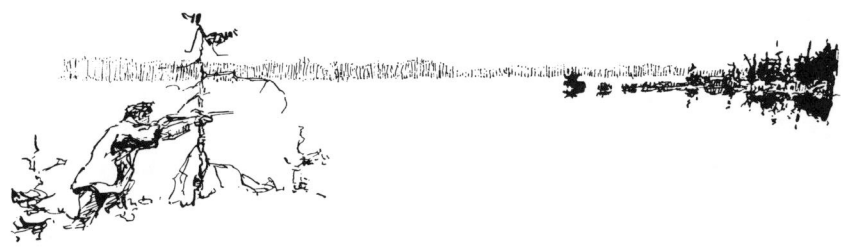

Chapter 10

PLUNDER

Nature looked sternly upon me for the murder of that moose.
Thoreau

My youngest brother, Lewis, was the scholar of the family. He was interested in poetry, philosophy, and foreign languages but not in blood sports. It must have been the unusually warm, sunny weather that led him to accept, at long last, an invitation to come with me on a hunting trip.

It was, indeed, a perfect Indian summer day as we pushed out into the Rat Root River. The tall hardwoods that lined the banks were in finest autumn foliage, with the reds and yellows in their branches repeating themselves in leaves that circled down to float in masses on the clear water.

That water, though, turned out to be less pure than it looked.

We used to tilt the paddle up and drink what ran off the blade wherever we happened to be. You might get your shirt wet but you wouldn't have to worry about getting sick. That happy situation was already changing. I knew well enough that, downstream from a settlement as we were, we really ought to boil the water for drinking. We didn't bother.

The next morning was too pleasant for good duck hunting and we were soon on our way, under a sun so warm that we pulled off first our canvas and woolen jackets and then our shirts and undershirts.

The Rat Root runs into one of several long bays that Rainy Lake pushes out, south and north, into both nations. Here I had a bright idea. "Let's set up the tent, leave this load of decoys, ammunition and cold weather gear in it, and head up over the border."

Lewis raised no objection. He was the guest, so I don't suppose I can shift any of the blame to him. This was the second bad mistake in twenty-four hours. An unhealthy average.

The canoe was sprightly, burdened only with a minimum of food, a blanket each, and very little other equipment. One item that I unwrapped from a canvas bundle caused Lew some surprise. It was a 30-army rifle.

"What do you expect to do with that thing? The season is closed in Minnesota. Do you have an Ontario hunting license?"

"Do you know what they charge a foreigner for a nonresident license? That's figured for rich, old sports. Besides, we won't really be hunting. It's just that we might need a little camp meat."

Lewis didn't say much, but enough to let me know that he didn't look with favor on that idea. He wasn't the outlaw type.

Continuing north over the long expanse of Redgut Bay I became aware that all was not well in my own gut. At sundown, on the portage into Lake Otukamamoan, cramps were bending me, and Lewis was not looking very good either. We were both going to pay for my indiscretion in not boiling the river water.

The weather was changing. The wind was out of the Northeast and it carried a sprinkle of cold rain.

Near the far end of the portage we found the rotted and roofless remains of a cabin. Enough of one corner was still standing to provide a little protection from the gathering storm. Weak and stumbling now, we propped the canoe against it, along with some hand-hewn, moss-covered planks.

We settled down in this well-ventilated shelter, each wrapped in a blanket. Soon fingers of sleet came poking in and then snow, searching for us, and finding us wherever we rolled or shifted.

I still don't feel like saying much about the next two days and nights. We were very sick. We were too weak to take care of ourselves or of each other, or even to keep the fire going. Everything was waterlogged: clothing, blankets, wood. I wouldn't be able to live through such a situation now. I'd die as dead as that fire died. Fortunately, this all happened before hypothermia had been invented.

On the third day, for some inexplicable reason, we were both able to stand up and walk around a little. With inner birch bark and some shaved-down pine twigs we got a fire started. Going for more wood I found that a partridge had been sent to sit on a branch and wait for me. To wait patiently while I stumbled back for the rifle. My hands were too shaky to aim for his head, and the big slug blasted his body. There was enough of him left to boil into a soup that we were able to drink and keep down. We still didn't want any of the bacon or the soak-soft hardtack.

After a night's rest by the fire and another partridge, we felt strong enough to start back. The portage was out of the question. We wouldn't be up to that effort. We'd have to put into Otukomamoan, follow its shore to the outlet, and go down the river to Redgut. Maybe we could run the rapids.

We had set the canoe in the lake and were about to load it when a movement near the opposite shore caught my eye. A bull moose had waded out and was feeding in the shallows, black as a big, burnt stump against the strip of pale rushes. I stood there, staring at him.

"Don't even think of it," said Lewis.

I got the rifle and bent to push out the canoe. Lewis stepped in and took his place to paddle while still advising me, in urgent whispers, to give up the project.

With a few strokes we slid behind a swampy point that ran out from the shore between us and the target. We kept low as we crossed the bay to this ambush, except that I raised a little from time to time for a look over the grass. At every peek I expected the moose to be gone, and almost hoped that he would be. But there he stood, usually with his head down, groping for under-water pasture.

When we reached the point I swung the stern against the shore, stepped out on quaking bog, and half waded, half crawled toward my prey. Sickness was suddenly gone, or forgotten in the excitement of the hunt. I stood up behind a dead swamp spruce and took aim, using its scrawny trunk to steady my hand.

It would be a long shot. For a guy that had burned up a lot of good ammunition in target practice and hunting, I was an outstandingly poor marksman. Usually. Almost always. But three times in my life I have aimed, to the best of this meager ability, at things that I really hoped to miss. On each of these occasions I have become, for just that moment, a deadeye sharpshooter.

I squeezed the trigger and the bull fell. I splashed back to the canoe. As we came around the point he got up and ran, away from us but parallel to the shore. Now I was in my usual shooting form. Taking my time, aiming carefully, I emptied the rifle, missing, and missing again. But at the fifth shot, the last in the rifle, he went down for keeps.

We were back in a bad situation. Worse than ever, you might say. Along with our bellyaches we now had an island of moose in knee-deep ice water. There was nothing to do but step out into it and go to work.

We had no axe or bone-saw: just our pocket knives. That would have been all right for the Northern Anishinabeg. Those expert anatomists can take any animal apart fast with just a sharp little blade. For us, the misery of that butchering went on for hours.

The heavy sky gave no hint of where the sun might be, but the day must have been well along when we hoisted the dripping, rolled-up hide and loaded it on top of the huge hams, shoulders, and other pieces that we had piled between the thwarts.

I looked at the canoe and shuddered. It was sitting so low in the water that even the little waves of this quiet afternoon were licking at the gunwales.

Again, there seemed to be no choice. We climbed into our places. Gradually we coaxed and bullied the sullenly resisting craft into clumsy motion.

At the end of the lake we got out, stood on the rocks, and looked glumly down at the first rapid. Impossible.

The portage around it was long and punishing. Neither of us was strong enough, yet, to handle one of those big slabs of meat alone. We cut a pole, slung one of them from it, and carried it between us, our knees sagging at every step.

In addition to the meat, I was carrying a new and increasing burden of guilt. All this heft, biting into my shoulder at every step, kept impressing on me that I had more to answer for now than an illegitimate pickerel. We wouldn't be let off this time with a scolding or a brown paper check. I had become conscious of the new morality: absolute obedience to the state, not from virtue but from fear of punishment.

The river, the rocks along its banks, and the forest above the rocks seemed empty of all life except our own. But we knew that a canoe could come around the bend below the rapid at any moment. So we set each load down in the concealment of a clump of tag alders while we went back for the next. We rested often and it took a long time.

We made it across a second portage that day but could go no farther. The weather had turned cold. A little dust of snow made white, lacy patterns on the dark stone and frozen earth. In the shelter of overhanging boulders we built a fire and fried some moose liver.

We felt better for a while. But this was to be another bad night. It was so cold that, even in our sleep, we kept working closer to the fire. Once I woke to find my blanket smoldering. In the morning there were holes scorched in our socks.

We were pretty well recovered from our stomach pains, though, and stronger than we had been the day before. We started at first light and bucked the wind down the long bay. The waves didn't find it hard to wash over the low-loaded gunwales. Lewis did as much bailing as paddling.

I was thinking about a group of official-looking buildings that we had passed on the way up. They flew the Union Jack and were situated at a point where the bay narrowed to river dimensions and current.

Not knowing what authority might be lodged in this outpost of the empire, we approached it with some concern. Better not pass it by daylight. We went ashore in an out-of- the-way cove, boiled some meat for supper, and waited for darkness.

We hoped that the wind would go down with the sun, as promised in the saying. That night was one of the frequent exceptions. Waves buffeted us in the big bay but diminished as we entered the shelter of the narrows. Snow was falling again. The water became a black passageway between white shores.

We came around the last bend and in sight of the post, then back-paddled in dismay. A broad shaft of light ran out from the main building, illuminating the whole river and the opposite bank.

Scouting closer, we found a narrow path of shadow where the light angled out a little from the pier. We sneaked into that trihedral darkness, almost scraping the planks on one side and bending low to stay out of the light on the other. Lewis had pulled in his paddle. I was using the silent Anishinabe hunting stroke, with blade turned edgewise in the forward movement and pushed through the water to avoid the sound of dripping on the surface.

All went well until we had passed the buildings and were approaching the end of the narrows. Then a bell screamed. A light came on over the boathouse. We dug hard at the water. Over my shoulder I caught a glimpse of a power boat coming down a ramp.

Slowly, painfully slowly, our heavily loaded canoe began to pick up speed. River spread into bay. Here in the open the wind and waves were strong again and the air was filled with flying snow.

White islands were coming at us out of the misty darkness ahead. We went into them like a rabbit into a briar patch. We didn't see the motor boat again. If the lawmen were really after us they must have known that they had little chance of catching anybody in that maze of rock, water, and driving snow.

But the guilty flee where no man pursueth. We had intended to hole up somewhere on the Canadian side and to stay off the main body of Rainy Lake until the wind went down.

Now we were too scared to stop. We came out of the islands, out of the bay, and into the open lake. In the darkness we could read neither map nor compass. We had no idea of where we were heading, no purpose except to leave avenging justice behind.

We soon had no choice but to run before the wind. A turn to either side would have brought the water pouring in over the narrow freeboard. Even on that course the waves were breaking over the stern, pounding against my back and down into the hull.

I shouted to Lewis to shove his paddle back into the meat and bail. Each time the stern lifted and the bow plunged, the water would come sloshing down in front of him, giving him depth for full buckets. He was tossing out a lot of it but a lot was coming in. I hoped that he could hold the pace. And I wished that there were some way to get that hard-won cargo over the side.

Flashes of white water shot up out of the darkness on our right. I ruddered hard. The canoe swung sharply round. The next wave came in, heavy, brutal, and icy, over the starboard side. Then we were in the lee of the island, maneuvering the flooded but right-side-up canoe toward a break in snow-covered rocks.

Soon our tattered blankets and holey socks were drying before a fire, and the upturned canoe was reflecting heat on our backs. We didn't know what country we were in, but we were safe, hidden and comfortable. We were going to stay like that until the storm was over.

When that time arrived we still weren't very strong. There was a long paddle to the Rat Root, and then against the current.

When we got to the settlement we were tired beyond all caution. In early afternoon we came alongside the dock and stacked the meat on it. The chunks were water-soaked gray on the outside but bright and red if you cut into them. They sat there on the public planks with the hairy, black hide, subject to the stares of every passerby for the next two hours while we first struggled to get the car started and, when we failed at that, went in search of a tow. Nobody paid any attention to the obviously illegal meat mound. But we had already been punished.

That was the most miserable trip that I ever had, and it was Lewis' only hunt. He told me later that, much as he had suffered, he wouldn't want to have missed the experience of going into a foreign country, committing a crime, and escaping over the border with the plunder.

"As for hunting," he went on, "I'm sure it's a delight to you masochists. But I can think of other forms of delinquency that I enjoy more."

Chapter 11

THE GALLEYS OF VENICE

> Blithely ran the wooden boat,
> Sped the boat, the journey quickened.
> Splash of oars was heard afar,
> Far the creaking of the oarlocks.
> The Kalevala

Sunsets over the harbor are a subject tempting to painters, but not easy. I advised the beginners in my landscape classes to choose something closer and more intimate. Like one of that row of piles standing up out there in the glowing water, each of them an outdoor still life. The old posts were tilted at odd angles, blackened by fire and crowned with growths of moss and weeds, quite beautiful in the evening light.

They were the only remains of the central palace and headquarters of the Duluth Boat Club, a wooden Venice that once spread out over St. Louis Bay. A few buildings left from its Oatka Branch are still in use farther out on the Point. But the lofty halls of the Spirit

Lake Branch, some ten miles up the river, have long ago moldered down into the surrounding mud and willows.

In my schooldays this majestic institution, with its docks, walkways, bridges, boathouses, indoor swimming pool, ballrooms, tennis courts, grandstands, dining halls, and dormitories, each rising gracefully above its reflection, seemed an eternal empire. Duluth's elite carried out their commercial and political negotiations over its polished tables, and their courtships on its dance floors and in its cushioned canoes. The city's proletariat crowded the long grandstands, waving blue and white pennants and cheering as the crews came battling down the course to the finish line. No college crowd that I saw in later years was more enthusiastic or more loyal.

My father had rowed at Harvard and at the Boat Club, setting a course that I followed eagerly but prematurely. At fifteen, I had become suddenly tall and spindly, not at all in the class with the slim but broad-shouldered Scandinavian types who made up most of the first and second crews. Nevertheless, I applied and was accepted for the squad.

I went each afternoon directly from high school to strain at the rowing machines in the sweat-fragrant YMCA basement. Then out into the winter twilight, jogging over steep and snowy streets, dodging the sleighs and the growing numbers of hoarse-honking automobiles.

Training was both Spartan and puritanical. As soon as the ice went out in the spring we moved down to the Point and into the living quarters provided by the club for its galley slaves. The trainers looked on women as a menace and took every precaution to protect us from their depredations. We were released during school and working hours. Otherwise we lived a life of poverty, chastity, and obedience, with special emphasis on the mortification of the flesh.

In the first morning light each crew stood beside its shell, a light, narrow boat, sixty feet long and sleek as a race horse. At the coxswain's command we lifted it from its rack, raised it above our heads, and carried it, on rigid arms, out of the boathouse. I could feel the rough grain of the planks, wet and often icy under my stockinged feet, as we stood waiting for the order to lower the boat into the water.

Then, as it lay beside the dock, each man slid his oar into the outrigger, eased himself down to the wheeled seat, reached out to close the oarlock, and laced his feet into the nailed-down shoes. No attention was paid to rain or snow, and seldom was practice canceled for wind.

In the afternoon we would be out there again bending our backs under the verbal flogging from the coaches' launch. Heartfelt cursing often became inadequate and might give way to colorful hyperbole.

"You there, Olson. I can piss more water in a minute than you pull in a week!"

Olson, Aakvik, Karlstrom—horned helmet names. I envied the targets of the invective. The lordly men with the megaphones didn't deign to waste their fury on Peyton.

After supper the old guys in their twenties might play a few hands of cards or discuss the standard conversational topic for single men of that age. The lights-out signal soon sent them to the dormitory where we smaller ones, exhausted, would already be asleep.

At this time the power and glory of the Duluth Boat Club were coming under attack from the all-devouring automobile. People began to drive out of the city, spending their spare time in cars rather than boats.

Memberships and donations slumped. The thick steaks for which the Club's training table had been noted gave way to thin stew. The heat in the dormitory was shut off completely at night to save fuel. Rowing clothes were sent less often to the laundry. This resulted in an epidemic of boils, most of them located at that vulnerable point where the tailbone bears down on the sliding seat.

In the cold morning dimness I found my trunks either damp and smelly from many workouts or frozen so stiff that I could hardly pull them on.

The seats rolled on steel tracks whose sharply angled ends were guarded by leather pads. These had a way of dropping off. With reduced maintenance they were not replaced. The sharp corners dug into my calves and then pounded black grease into the sores, leaving tattoo marks that showed for many years.

We grumped about such discomforts, but there was no talk of mutiny. I'm not sure whether we were more hardy than today's athletes or just more docile.

I was younger than my shipmates, gawky, timid, and incapable of either smooth rowing or easy conversation. Naturally I was at the bottom of the social order, a position that was likely to have uncomfortable consequences in this primitive brotherhood.

Walking one night over the high and crookedly angular bridge from dining hall to dormitory, I heard voices behind me: then I became aware that I was the subject of a heated argument.

"I'll take the left leg."

"Oh no you won't. You had that on the last one. I'll take the left leg and you can have a wing."

I walked faster, but they kept pace, settled their differences, and laid hands on me. Each, I assume, seized his agreed portion.

"One—two—three" and I was airborne, arching high, then splashing deep into dark water. I swam to a floating dock and climbed out in time to hear the jocular voices departing. All of us were supposed to know how to swim. They hadn't asked me but had stayed long enough to make sure.

ଓଆଠ

"There be some sports are painful and their labor sets them off."

Maybe Shakespeare had rowed in a boat race. There were some good ones in his time. It is a painful pleasure.

My father put the same idea in different words. It was before my racing days started. He and I were in a canoe on the bay, approaching the empty bleachers.

"By the time you get to this point," he remarked, "you are wondering how you ever got yourself into such a damn fool game."

It was a strong statement for a man who seldom used profanity. Not many years later I learned exactly what he meant. When your breath is gone, your lungs are burning, and your middle is breaking in two, that is when you must pull harder than ever.

Duluth crews had developed a unique way of psyching themselves into a spurt at this exhausted moment. Slugging down the last half mile, behind the other boat, someone would utter a wordless animal howl, the roar of the Viking ancestors. Others would answer. Suddenly a mystic unity would be established. The flagging combative ferocity would be restored. You could feel the shell shoot ahead.

You dared not turn your head, but from the corner of your eye you would catch a glimpse of the rival rudder. Then you would see their coxswain, screaming, pounding with his wooden rope grips as he watched the lead narrow. Next, one by one, the silently straining oarsmen would come into view. The finish buoy would flash past and we would slump forward, gasping over our oars. Either we had won the race or we had given a better crew a bad scare.

The Boat Club, as I knew it, is long dead. Water sports, depressed for years, have made a striking comeback. Power boats roar louder than the old crews as they rip the bay, leaving a bold, manly, carcinogenic mist. Surfers maneuver across the white rollers of a

northeaster. On quiet summer evenings, a graceful fleet with multi-colored sails spreads itself over the lake. Each sailboat has a motor ready for emergencies, so they dare to go far from the canal. The oarsmen and oarswomen of another Duluth rowing club look smooth and swift in their shells. But they are no longer feared by eastern crews. They have not reestablished the old supremacy.

Maybe Duluth oarspersons should roar again.

Chapter 12

WATERS OF ACADEME

> *Gaudeamus igitur iuvenes dum summus.*
> Therefore let us rejoice while we are young.
> Traditional

"Who's your room mate?"

"Peyton."

"That dumb shit?"

"He's right in the next room, for Christ's sake."

"Oh! Sorry."

That brief appraisal, heard through an open door, seemed to pretty well summarize my standing at Phillips Exeter Academy. I felt sure that it represented the opinion of all my richer, smarter, and more sophisticated classmates. That is to say, all my classmates. This increased my tendency to keep quiet and keep to myself. I escaped attention by acting even dumber than I really was.

The Academy was said to be the easiest prep school to get into and even easier to get kicked out of. The policy was not to be choosy about admissions but, after that, to let natural selection take its course. A considerable proportion of each freshman class was invited not to come back from Christmas vacation.

After three undistinguished years at high school I had transferred to PEA. With an optimism common to low-grade students I believed, during my first month there, that I was working hard and probably doing quite well.

That comfortable misapprehension ended when my faculty adviser called me into his study to give me my grades. These consisted of one just-barely-passing and four flunks. His cool, professional, last-chance warning was hardly necessary. I was scared. From then on, I took time out from studying for eating, sleeping, and daily exercise, but for almost nothing else.

In the first swimming tryouts there were many better than I in every event. When rowing started I was assigned a place on the fourth boat.

For a few days I was rushed by my father's old fraternity, then dropped, as soon as my true character was understood and my mental and physical limitations recognized.

Somehow I survived athletic, social and scholastic disgrace and, after two long, hard years, graduated. Before that event the brothers of Kappa Epsilon Pi swallowed hard and took me in.

Initiations had gotten out of the Academy's control. Ours was long, painful, and degrading, obviously designed by youthful but imaginative sadists. Fortunately it was administered by normal guys, most of whom had enough sense to ease up a little at the worst points. But during its course I became so prudishly and obnoxiously uncooperative that I fully expected to be refused admission.

My moderately merciful tormentors didn't go that far. I signed the sacred document in my own blood and assumed the duties and privileges of the order. When I learned, a few days later, that acceptance is an unbreakable rule for any son of a former member, I was so humiliated that I rejected even the kindest attempts to engage me in fraternal activities.

In my opinion Exeter is a fine school. I am grateful for what it gave me. But I was always acutely conscious of my lowly status there until one touch of glory came in the final weeks.

A liberal critic of eastern preparatory schools called their products "bogus little English gentlemen." Without entirely accepting that judgment, I will admit that British precepts of silent effort and the stiff upper lip were followed on the playing fields of Exeter and also on the winding surface of the Swampscott River where it widens out to meet the salt water below the town. The coxswains screamed and hammered there, as those noisy little simians do everywhere, but the oarsmen toiled in silence.

At the end of my second year on the river I was at stroke oar on the second crew. We were coming in every day in a properly humble position behind the heavier and better coordinated varsity. We had been trying hard all that spring, but had been unable to reduce their lead.

One afternoon as we approached the finish line in our customary trailing position, I had an impulse to roar, Norse fashion, and did.

The coxswain, silent for once, stared at me with eyes and mouth wide open. The coach, equally astonished, lowered his megaphone. There was no response from my shipmates. I realized that my song would not be appreciated without a libretto.

"Come on! Let's get 'em!" I speeded the cadence of the stroke.

Somehow the message got through. There was no answering bellow, as there would have been on St. Louis Bay, but I could feel the surge of new power. We came up on the other boat, man by man, in the old, familiar way and crossed the finish line a tidy half length ahead.

The next day and each day thereafter there were rematches, always with the same result. So the numbers of the boats were reversed and I ended my career as varsity stroke.

I wish I could report that we won our final race, but the Middlesex crew was too fast to be overcome by yelling. All the same I strutted proudly when I received my sweater. The aggressively modest convention of the time required that it be worn inside out, so that the red E was facing my chest. But the stitches that held it in place were clearly visible.

The fact that I was still a dumb shit was now unimportant. I had redeemed myself in the eyes of the brothers. But I was unable to relax or become sociable among them. That would have taken more time than was left.

ogso

At Yale I was as hopelessly outclassed in crew as I had been in swimming at Exeter. But water polo came easy. It was a roughneck game with no holds barred, quite different from the ladylike sport played by today's college students. I will record just one memory of it here.

A Princeton forward had the ball and I had the forward. The other players were churning the water around us, his teammates struggling to come to the rescue and mine to hold them off.

In the center of this turmoil he and I were peacefully entwined. My arms were locked around his head and my legs were comfortably scissored around his middle. We were near the Princeton side of the pool, rising and falling in gentle rhythm. Each time we came to the surface I was getting a good supply of air, and he, in the lower position, was getting nothing.

I have no bias whatever against Princeton men. I always make a point of being friendly to them, and I have known several who were really quite nice. But among their less attractive characteristics is a certain obstinacy. All the fellow had to do was to let go of the ball and I would have been off his back and far away. I was in no hurry, though. He could hang on to it as long as he pleased.

As my face came up again out of the water I saw a strange apparition. A white-haired old gentleman was crouched at the edge of the pool, striking at me with a furled umbrella. He leaned far out. The tip splashed close to my head. But I was still untouched as we descended below the water.

The next time we rose I looked anxiously over my shoulder. Two officials were dragging the old guy back to his seat in the bleachers. I have since wondered whether he was a relative of the man below or just a loyal Princeton alumnus.

I don't remember whether my stubborn opponent finally gave up the ball or whether his friends broke through and pulled me off.

⊂₃₈⊃

At this time I was courting a girl in New York about whom I will have considerably more to say later. When studies or polo practice kept me in town on Saturday I would get up early the next morning, buy a special low-rate ticket, and squeeze into the ancient excursion train which, at two dollars and twelve cents per head, carried a presumably underprivileged and certainly unwashed cargo of New Haveners down the coast for a day in the big city.

The regularity of these visits did not pass my teammates unnoticed. Every such group has its funny man, and ours made his comment one afternoon in the locker room.

"Peyton's got to be getting a pretty fancy piece of ass to go chasing off like that every weekend."

Incredible as it may seem in this age of enlightenment, I was getting sweet kisses, pleasant feminine companionship, and that was all. But instead of accepting the kidding in the cordial spirit in which it was offered, I reacted in a hostile manner.

"She's a nice girl. Not like the kind you go around with. So shut up."

After one of these Sunday trips I developed a powerful itch in an inconvenient location. At the University dispensary it was quickly diagnosed as crabs.

In case you don't happen to be acquainted with these affectionate little creatures, informally known as pants-rabbits, they are undersized lice that inhabit pubic hair. They prefer dirty people but may be willing to make an exception for an occasional clean one, even one who spends a couple of hours a day in the pool. They come to you either by sexual contact or by some other intimate connection with one of their steady hosts or hostesses. Such as, I reasoned, sitting on a still-warm seat cushion.

The sad condition of the New York, New Haven and Hartford Railroad, like that of the Duluth Boat Club, had been brought about by the demon automobile. I started to explain this to the doctor as the reason for its filthy seat cushions and so for my louse colony. He didn't seem much interested. He shaved and anointed me and gave instructions for further action against late-hatching crab infants.

That took care of my guests. But a further embarrassment had to be faced. Our polo practice was conducted without suits.

I walked into the pool area and up to the waiting squad as though nothing had changed. Perhaps my new baldness would be tactfully disregarded.

Vain hope. The swimming team, who were just leaving, stopped chattering and stretched their scraggy necks to get a better view. A chorus of whoops came from the polo benches and then the smart remarks.

"Little boys your age are not allowed in the pool without their mothers."

"Hadn't you heard? That's the new Minnesota haircut."

More sympathetic comments and inquiries were almost equally unwelcome. I suggested that it was time to get on with the practice, but that seemed to be impossible until everybody had received complete information.

At last the inquisition ended and we crouched, knees bent, toes hooked over the edge of the pool, waiting to be released by the toss of the ball. At this tense moment the jester remarked, thoughtfully, "A guy sure has to be careful with those nice girls."

Chapter 13

SINGING IN THE WILDERNESS

> And thou beside me, singing in the wilderness,
> Ah, wilderness were paradise enow.
>
> Omar Kayyam

My grandfather married a girl from across the bay in Superior. So did my father. And I was conscientious about carrying out family traditions.

I had met Fay at a Christmas party in her home town. She was already familiar with the world beyond Wisconsin. She had studied piano in Paris, played with a Philadelphia Symphony quartet, and was a member of a professional dance group in New York. When the vacation ended she returned to that city and I to Yale.

I had been warned by experienced classmates about the expense of taking a girl out in New York. Some boasted that they had spent $50 in one night. I didn't believe that, but I did go that first time mentally and financially prepared for a big splurge at the elaborate shows and nightclubs of the prohibition era.

Fay had other ideas about entertainment. On this and subsequent dates we went to art galleries, dance recitals, concerts and museums, ate at little ethnic restaurants, and visited with people who were doing things in the arts.

Inspired by Italian renaissance paintings, Isadora Duncan had broken away from the restrictions of classic ballet, and New York had become the center for the modern dance. We saw the great ones—Page, St. Dennis, Kreutsberg, Graham—and many enthusiastic younger dancers, each with ideas of his or her own contributions to the new art. A fine performance might be given before a small audience in a warehouse loft, or in somebody's apartment.

It was all very different from, and a lot more exciting than, the New York I had known before. Ignorant as I was, I could see that something bold and good was getting started. Those weekends, or more often Sundays, were a new experience in my life, even though I was understanding only a little of what I was seeing.

I had pretty well stopped my drawing and painting, having acquired the notion that there was something unmanly about it. Fay brought me back to it with encouraging words and the gift of a fine set of English watercolors.

In New Haven, too, pearls were being slopped into my trough by dedicated teachers. Occasionally I would snuffle one up: they made my college experience worth the time and money. But most of them I just stomped into the mud.

One evening I had gone to the apartment of a young instructor in English for help with a passage from *King Lear*. He answered my questions, translating and explaining the powerful, archaic language, until I got the full meaning.

"Now that you understand it," he said, "isn't it wonderful? Doesn't it stir you?"

I answered with stupid honesty, "No, I can't say that it does."

Later, when I had gained some degree of appreciation, I regretted that inconsiderate reply.

CR80

A member of a varsity team, no matter how uncouth, naive, or solitary, could not be relegated to the untouchable caste. Thus my social standing at Yale never quite sank to the absolute zero that it had reached at Exeter. But it was plenty far down there. I was one of that oppressed majority, the non-fraternity barbarians.

Fraternities were big stuff at the colleges of those status-obsessed times. Each of them had its rating. This classification—prominent, satisfactory, or undesirable—was likely to be applied to its members. Any girl you met at a dance would ask you what fraternity you belonged to. The question was supposed to flatter, with its assumption that of course such a big, important man must be a member of *some* fraternity. When I confessed that this was not my case I could always see my stock plummet.

I had politely refused the one fraternity bid that had been offered me. I knew, from past experience, that membership would be of no use to me, nor would it be for the good of the order.

In spite of this humble standing I was to have my little triumph at Yale, just as I finally had at Exeter. Only this time it would happen, not on or in the water, but, of all places, on the ballroom floor.

When Fay came up for the prom, a contrary class prevented my escorting her to the early afternoon parties. I asked Bill Smith, a dormitory neighbor, to take her to the first tea dance.

I had finally been turned loose and was hustling across the campus to take over, when I was halted by another dweller in our dorm well. "Just wait till you see Smith's classy little blonde! And what a dancer! Maybe you can get a dance with her. But I doubt it."

Without taking time to explain, I hurried on. I was eager to relieve Mr. Smith of his responsibility. For the rest of the weekend I basked at the focus of reflected glory.

Since I had no connections with the Yale beau monde, and since that distinguished group of young gentlemen had no prior knowledge of my date, I hadn't been able to get anybody's name on my program for the final evening formal. I needn't have worried. As soon as my partner's looks and dancing had been displayed I suddenly became sought after. I was unskilled in that situation and exchanged so many dances that she mildly reproached me for not having saved more for myself.

When the festivities were over and the guests had departed I was the subject of puzzled envy. The question was being asked—sometimes, with the candor of youth, in my presence—how could a guy like Peyton get a girl like that?

I hadn't got her yet. That project would still need considerable promotion. At nineteen she had every prospect of a bright career either as a dancer or as a concert pianist. Looking back, I have been shaken by the selfishness of my persistence in asking her to give up these prospects and settle down as the wife of a small town businessman.

Although I had come to respect interpretive dancing and to enjoy the recitals, I had no aptitude for her arts. So she adopted mine. She took a drawing course with Kimon Nicolaides, whose "Natural Way to Draw" has since become a standard text book in art schools.

Having this interest in common meant a lot to us in the years that followed. Gerry Pierce, the Arizona watercolorist, once said to us, "You fortify each other." It can be distressing for a non-artist to be tied to somebody who may, at any moment, be seized with the overwhelming necessity to hold everything, stop the car or boat, and paint some magic mountain or shanty. The only defense is to get out your own sketchbox and go at it too.

ଓଞ୍ଚଠ

It has been suggested that couples contemplating marriage should first camp together. If they can endure each other for a couple of weeks in the woods they should be able to get along under civilized conditions for the rest of their lives.

I note that some of my young friends are now taking this precaution, and I wish them success. Back in those dark ages it was just a funny saying.

Naturally, our honeymoon was a canoe trip. Fay had never gone in for this sort of travel, but she learned fast. As soon as we had landed for the night she would be busy. By the time that I had put the tent up and brought in the wood supply, she would have laid out the bedding, built the fire, filled the water bucket, and started cooking.

She didn't holler if the mosquitoes were so thick that they got into the porridge, or if we had to sleep on that worst of all beds, slanting rocks. And when we stopped to consider some wind-swept lake crossing or roaring rapid, if anybody chickened out, it was I.

A severe test came that first autumn of our marriage, when we had moved to Ashland, an old-time mining and logging town on the Wisconsin shore. We had paddled down the Bad River and camped on Lake Superior.

In the morning Fay was introduced to duck hunting. The weather was at its worst: cold, driving, relentless rain. By noon we had acquired two small, careless ducks and were skin-soaked and bone-chilled.

Way off across the marshes we could see smoke whipping away from the tin stovepipe of a shack. We paddled and waded our way to it and entered, dripping puddles on the clay floor. Two Indian trappers lived there. One of them built up the fire for us. The other, lifting his head from under a pile of quilts, said, "I bet you wish you was where I am," and sank back out of sight.

We dried our clothes and warmed our shivering selves. The hours passed. The rain beat steadily on the roof. I had to be at work the next morning. There was nothing for it but to leave this comfortable place and head up the river.

Back in our flat, Fay reported the discovery of one dry spot in her woolen underwear. It was located under her belt buckle and was the size of a silver dollar. She further stated that she had never been that cold in her life.

But we went duck hunting again the next weekend. For thirty-five years after that she was with me, barring pregnancies, on every camping trip.

Although not specifically selected for aquatic talent she took to our family's swimming enthusiasm. She could give my brothers and me a good race on the surface. She would swim so far under water that more than once I began to wonder whether she was ever going to come up. I'd be just about to go in after her when she'd appear far beyond the area that I'd been watching.

On summer canoe trips we always worked in at least one swim a day, and in hot weather there might be several. As the weather got colder, extreme cleanliness seemed, to me, less essential. But she carried the early morning dip far into autumn while I watched, in well-bundled admiration, from the shore.

Ever since childhood I had expected and required extreme hardihood in my companions. If one of them complained, or even looked too obviously miserable when he was tired, cold, or hungry, I was unlikely to go out with him another time. In this way I established an elite corps of one—Chink—gradually increased, in later years, by a few others who qualified for the pleasure of my company.

Then, as now, there were a large number of young ladies in the world. How extraordinary that I met and married one of them who, never having lived this kind of life before, not only endured it but enjoyed even the worst of it as though she had been brought up in an igloo.

When we moved back to Minnesota we would spend November weekends on Third River. By then a road had been built to that stream. This improvement eliminated the mud-and-sand run but required drastic measures to beat out the competition.

In the last twilight of a November evening we stamped and kicked a path through the ice of the reedy margin to where the river flowed. From there we paddled downstream, past the fires of many hunters camped in the protection of the forest, and along channels through the marshland to where the swamp shores fell away and wild rice stems, now free of the weight of grain, tapped audibly against the hull of our canvas canoe. Then out into the silent sky and water until the beam from our tin-can lantern, prodding through the falling snow ahead, found a flat streak, white in the darkness.

This was the island. At least it was an island now that the lake level was low—a gravel bar, maybe fifty feet long. It was not a good camp site: small, damp, devoid of firewood, and the target of all the winds that blew across Winnebigoshish. But it was the strategic spot at the center of the estuary where almost every flock would swing low as it followed the river to the bay and then curved out over the lake.

Hunters of earlier times had piled stones here to form a blind. In this poor shelter we spread a canvas tarp, laid out on it a bundle of straw that we had brought with us, and bound the canoe in place overhead as a roof against the snow. Sleeping a little, shivering more, we got through the night.

Long before dawn, the first flashlight came searching for the island, showing double in the calm water of this early hour. I called out a good morning greeting, trying not to let the gloat sound in my voice. The boat turned back to seek some lesser blind along the shore. Soon there were others, each intent on being the first to reach the island. As we fended them off we ate a cold breakfast, dished out with mittened hands. We were ready at first light for the familiar, but always thrilling, whistle of wings overhead.

Several of my earlier partners had camped with me here. Only Chink and Fay were willing to come back to it again.

⊗

Another year and a colder November night on the island. Neither of us could sleep. Cramps knotted my leg muscles. I was getting old.

No lights came over the water.

The predawn glow showed a pale expanse of ice covering the bay and stretching far out into the lake. A dark pool remained open at one end of the bar. This was the situation that a duck hunter dreams about. But I was worried.

When the morning flight slacked off we picked up the decoys and loaded them, along with ducks, guns, ammunition and other heavy articles, well back toward the stern. Fay sat in the middle. The rolled tarp and blankets, bulky but light, went in front leaving the bow well up in the air.

We poked this elevated snout up over the ice and were relieved to feel the surface give way under us with no sound of tearing canvas. Cautiously, laboriously, we crunched a path to where the impatient river was still holding a channel open for us.

Since then I've wondered how it would have been if the ice had been too thick to break. I suppose we'd have had to wait until it was thick enough to walk over. We wouldn't have starved but we'd have been good and sick of raw bluebill.

Chapter 14

BANKING AND BIRTHING

> To hell with this United States! I'm going back to Minnesota.
>
> A Norse settler

When we were not on forest excursions, Fay and I worked hard. We came to Ashland in July 1930. The depression was not quite at its worst but was rapidly getting there. Fay gave lessons in dancing and piano, stirring up a lively interest in these arts, and doing considerably better in her business than I did in mine. That small enterprise was staggering under the weight of the hard times.

So were the banks. Bringing in a modest deposit one morning I found a group of excited people buzzing around the locked door. In those days we all knew what that meant. I was glad that I had taken the girl's advice.

The hired girl (usually spoken of as just "the girl," regardless of her age) is now an extinct species in middle class America, but then even a poor family had to have one. Fay paid ours out of her lesson income, thus buying time to give the classes. This particular girl, or cook, or maid, also proved to be a capable financial consultant. She had passed on to me the rumor that the Northern National was in bad shape. To guard against its failure, and also because I needed the money, I had slyly borrowed from the bank a larger sum than we had on deposit.

The last laugh was on me. A letter from the Federal Reserve Bank informed me that they had bought my note and that I should now send the payments to them.

Could they get away with a trick like that? They could and did. Eventually I had to pay off the note. Years later we got back a small percentage of our deposit. Don't let anybody tell you that it can't happen again.

Back home in Minnesota, too, banks were failing. Governor Floyd Olson, viewed by our family as close to a bomb-slinging bolshevik, was looking for a tough banker to clean up the state's shaken financial industry. He asked my father's brother to become commissioner of banks.

Uncle John was astonished. "But I'm a Republican," he told Olson. "I voted against you."

"Never mind that," the governor replied. "You take care of the banks and I'll handle the politics."

This was during the 1933 moratorium, when all the banks in the country were closed. Uncle John's duty was to separate the quick from the dead and to make sure that the survivors reopened on a sound basis.

When this work was finished he moved on to the chairmanship of my old adversary, the Federal Reserve Bank of Minneapolis. To qualify for this job he had to get rid of his bank stock, not a fast-selling item that season. My father bought his interest in a Duluth bank and asked me to come in as cashier and teller. I did, with the understanding that my stay would be temporary. Fay and I had decided to cut loose from city life and move to the woods. First, though, we needed some money.

Hard times were hanging on, but a feeling of optimism was in the air. The Peyton banks had come through, battered but solvent, still independent and family-owned. Foreclosed property could now at last be sold at some price, and many pastdue loans could be collected, a few dollars at a time, from men who were working again.

I was put in charge of investments, with authority to buy or sell as I thought advisable. It seemed a frightening responsibility for one who was completely inexperienced in this field, and who was personally flat broke. I felt better about it after I had talked to several other bankers and had come to realize the extent of their ignorance of the subject.

I had taken a course in stocks and bonds at Yale, and another on trusts. I had not been very good in these subjects and remembered them only dimly. All the same, what little of them had stuck with me made me feel quite knowledgeable in comparison to my counterparts in other banks.

The bright, young investment specialists who had given such convincing and ruinous advice in the twenties were gone now, and most small bankers preferred to fumble their own way through investment mysteries rather than to depend again on outside experts.

Some very sick bonds were, by this time, beginning to make gratifying recoveries, and others that had seemed hopeless were being watched eagerly for signs of life.

Our purchase of the bank had included a batch of Imperial Russian Governments, issued by the Czar and repudiated by the Soviets. These would usually trade at around three dollars a hundred, but every so often a rumor would get around that the Russians were buying them up, and they might bounce to ten or fifteen. I sold ours at one of those highs and was glad later that I had.

Our State of Arkansas road bonds, also in default, had not looked much better then the Russkis. We hung on to them and at last they were made good, in spite of passionate speeches in that state's legislature to the effect that Arkansas citizens were going hungry while the bankers were getting paid—a sort of preview of the future problems of the third world.

My personal financial position had been almost as bad as Arkansas'. Post-depression bank salaries were low, and mine was further reduced by my erratic performance at the counter. The coldly logical rule then in effect required a teller to make good any shortages, or any bad checks cashed, out of his own pocket. The trouble was that too often there was nothing in the pocket.

Maybe I was thinking of international finance as I pushed back the bond ledger and turned to make change for some customer at my window. I would often be there at night, searching through debits and credits, counting the cash over and over, and straining to remember which of the day's transactions might have led me astray.

At 7 PM I would call the Canton Cafe across the street and have them send over a sandwich. It might be close to midnight before I either found what I was looking for or gave up trying.

Paydays were settlement dates for this gambling account. Usually the bank paid me a few dollars, but sometimes I had to give it an IOU to stay in the game.

One purpose of this system was to keep the tellers careful, and it certainly had that effect on me. I counted every payment three times and called each bank on which a check was drawn to make sure that it was good. Quite often some payee in a hurry would start snorting and swearing over these delays. Then I figured that he might be trying to hustle me and that I'd better give the deal one more recount.

This caution began to pay off. My losses were brought under control, at least to the extent that we could buy our boy a Christmas present.

൜

Hamilton had been born properly in a hospital. His sister, Beryl, arrived during the night in a blizzard that blocked the streets with drifts and brought all traffic to a frozen halt.

I phoned the doctor and the nurse. They promised to come as soon as they could get through. Until then we would be as isolated as though we were in some cabin back in the bush.

Fay's first delivery had been so swift that she had barely made it to the hospital in time. In preparation for this next one she had sent to Washington for a how-to-do-it bulletin, published, appropriately, by the Department of Labor.

Reading from this book between pain spasms, she gave me instructions. I washed my hands, put clean sheets on the bed, and went back into the bathroom for the specified final ten minutes of hand-scrubbing.

Just at that point I heard the call. "Come now."

"As soon as I finish scrubbing."

"There won't be time for any more scrub . . ."

The summons was interrupted by a shuddering groan. The baby was on its way for sure, and in a hurry.

Then began one of several nightmarish occasions when I have known quiet, terrifying desperation. Each time I have gone on working calmly and to the best of my ability, but with the realization that events had gotten beyond my skill or knowledge. Survival, mine or somebody else's, was now about to be decided by luck, fate, or heaven. In this case the decision hung there for the next several hours.

Correction: Fay, checking this manuscript for errors, says that it was ten minutes. She has to be right. I forgot to look at the clock when we started.

The terse instructions of the bulletin covered only the preparations. It was obviously assumed that somebody who knew something would take over the actual delivery. All I had to go by were half-remembered stories, vague now, and puzzling.

Fortunately, matters were proceeding without action by me.

The top of the baby's head appeared. Then, after a tearing effort, the whole head. At that point, all progress came to a stop.

I was looking down into a tiny, wizened, upside-down face. It looked to me like a little blue monkey.

Was this a human being? Could it be ours? And what was I to do now?

Blue! Some memory came to my tormented consciousness that the color was a warning of suffocation. Strangling.

I know now that an untrained attendant is not supposed to pull. I didn't know it then.

I took hold of the head and pulled a little. Then harder. No results. I pulled as hard as I dared and called on Fay to bear down. The baby popped out like a cork from a bottle.

For a moment it lay there, silent, slimy, squirming, like some little reptile winkled out of the rocks.

Even I knew what should come next: the traditional and appropriate initiation to an unkind world. I picked her up by the feet and gave her a sharp spank. She responded with a strong and tension-breaking howl. She was breathing now.

The right move for a blue monkey. But what a way to welcome a lady who would eventually become a gracious and beautiful grandmother!

The nurse came stomping in out of the night, all crusted with snow. She had waded on foot through the drifts and the wind. Before she was out of her coat she was giving orders like a major-general. It was a blessed relief just to be doing what I was told.

A greater relief came when the most pressing chores had been completed and she told me that mother and daughter had come through in good shape. It was hard to believe that I hadn't done serious damage to one or the other.

Chapter 15

TIMBER FARM

> Emerson preached nature; Thoreau embraced nature; it is Thoreau, of course who ultimately strikes us as dangerous.
>
> Gruckow

We decided that we would move to the woods, catch or raise our own food, cut our own fuel, and educate our own children while getting what small amounts of cash we needed from writing and art work. It was a pretty good idea and I have never regretted attempting it, but it had weaknesses that quickly became apparent.

We took some good canoe trips to appraise prospective locations. I had to admit to myself, though, that living off the country was getting impossible, even for Indians. I began to count more on raising food than catching it. I was studying government bulletins on farming, and soon came to realize that carrying all the necessary supplies over portages would not be feasible.

So we compromised on a site in the hills above Duluth, a home place in the woods. Now it's a wooded place in a city.

I was influenced by happy memories of the old plantation in West Virginia. But on this farm there would be no cabins in the hollow, no corps of retainers to do the heavy work.

The first of many imperative demands was a trail from the road. The axe work went well enough. After that it was time to fill the low spots with gravel.

The wedding gift from my parents had been a Chevrolet coupe. I had specified that it be equipped with rumble seat, a fashionable feature of that time, consisting of a lid in the tail of the car that lifted up to make room for two passengers. I soon replaced this with a wooden box, less dashing in appearance but more practical for moving our kind of cargo, especially gravel.

The muddy trail swallowed amazing quantities of this material. The shovel was somehow less gracious than the paddle. There were no breaks for swimming or fishing and no changing scenery to break the monotony.

I was resting, puffing, and leaning on my shovel in such a way as to avoid pressing the handle against blistered palms when I saw a man walking toward me. A tall, lean man of about my own age, the late twenties. He was carrying a shovel.

He went to work silently but efficiently, moving considerably more gravel than I. I was relieved to have this assistance, but suspicious. "What's in it for him?" I wondered. "What does this guy really want?" I was unfamiliar with country customs.

The box was soon empty. We climbed aboard and started for the gravel pit. He told me that he was Hilmer Halverson, my nearest neighbor.

Hilmer had a job in Duluth, but after work he would often come over with his shovel or axe. His advice was as helpful as his labor.

A friend from Ashland who had had some experience as a carpenter helped me get a house up. It was a little house that sat on cedar posts instead of a basement. We moved in before it was finished.

Hilmer assured me that somewhere down below us, maybe fifteen feet, maybe forty, was bedrock. When a well shaft reached that foundation there would usually be a fairly adequate flow of good water. Any squirts that broke in higher up must be viewed with suspicion. They might turn out to be surface stuff that would have a strange taste and might dry up in time of drought. For this reason wells here were usually dug in winter when the water level

was at its lowest. But the digging would take time, and it was not too early to start. In the mean time we could get water from his pump.

The first step was to have the site tested and approved by a reliable witch. I was skeptical, but figured, as some do about prayer, that it couldn't do any harm and might help. And there was satisfaction in seeing the hand-held willow stick twitch strongly downward.

For the first three or four feet the digging was easy. From there on down was hardpan: each chunk had to be loosened with a pickaxe and then hacked out with a short-handled shovel.

At this point I remembered the local saying that if you want your wife to go out with other guys, use a short-handled shovel. It does leave you worn out at night. But there's no choice of weapons in a well-shaft.

When the well deepened Hilmer helped, hauling up the dirt in a bucket and sometimes spelling me at the digging. As a city boy I don't think I'd have made it without his farm-gained skill, technical advice, and encouragement.

At fourteen feet we hit a rock too big to move, or even to budge. I refused to think of starting over. I braced the rock with poles and kept on going down. This left an overhang that terrified me at first but that I finally accepted.

It was dark down there below that projection, and cold and wet. Dirt and water kept dribbling down on my head. Underneath was a sloshing layer of liquid mud. But the makeshift cribbing held and the big rock stayed in place. At thirty-five feet a strong vein of water came pouring in. I don't remember how long the job took except that it was a lot of weeks. Nobody who hasn't spent time moving dirt with pick and shovel has any idea how long it takes.

Our first winter on the farm, with the house on stilts and still uninsulated, was the coldest of my before-and-after life. I had nailed a thermometer to the north wall. Its mercury tube was held in place by a metal band that blocked out the readings from 50 to 54 below zero. One morning I found the tube white and clear, way down into that covered area. When, after several weeks like that, the weather eased up to twenty below, Fay said that it seemed like a heat wave.

Spring came, and I spaded in a garden between the stumps. Hilmer told me there'd be no use planting before Memorial Day, but I did anyway. Everything froze and had to be replanted. After that the corn shot up like rockets and the potato vines covered the ground. The stuff seemed to know that it had to hurry if it was ever going to amount to anything.

I got a little walking tractor. As a safety measure, it was designed to shut off if the handles were released. When it hit a tough root or a rock, the handles would lift, and I would put all my weight on them to hold them down and keep the thing running. When the plow found something really solid and I hung on too long it would hoist me over the motor, set me on my head in front of the tractor and conk out.

I kept this unruly little machine in the space under the house. One evening, as I was backing it down and in, it trapped me against the wall with its handles under the sill, so that they could not lift to kill the motor. I got out one loud bellow. Then the wheels just kept on rolling, grinding the crossbar against my chest. Fay came running from the house. Acting on my gasped instructions, she shut off the motor and shifted it into neutral. It had been a heavy squeeze, but ribs and tractor were undamaged.

In time we got chickens, ducks, geese and milk goats. The goats were a Swiss breed, and mostly hornless. One timid little doe had horns. Gradually she became bolder and eventually became the boss goat. She butted her sisters away from the feed. I took to spreading grain out in a long skein on the snow to give everybody a chance. The queen ran back and forth chasing the others away from the feed. While she was battering them back at one end, though, some bold ones would be sneaking in for a quick grab at the other. Soon all the feed would be gone and the royal goat had gotten none.

To keep her from starving to death I sawed off her horns. After that every goat that got near her would take a bunt at her, even little kids that had been born after her deposition.

This was several decades before the back-to-the-land movement became fashionable. Society was not so permissive as it has since become. A sincere disgust at my quitting the business race was soon made evident, perhaps with a little secret envy for our freedom. Contemptuous words were relayed to us or sometimes came floating back from departing guests who thought themselves out of earshot.

It was assumed that I had dragged Fay into the wilderness against her wishes. That didn't exempt her from criticism. "What's the matter with the *girl*? She must be a dishrag."

We scorned these comments, but they may have affected my thinking. Also, we needed more money. I lacked the resolution of a

Gaugin, a Van Gogh, or a Modigliani. I never quite achieved the true artist's contempt for middle class values.

I cleared and fenced more land and took on operations beyond our subsistence intentions. We sold poultry and eggs in the city and hatched chicks, ducklings and goslings for sale to the rural community that was growing around us. At night I did illustrations for small publications and wrote magazine articles.

Not much time was left in those early years for easel painting or canoeing. But years passed swiftly. Our children began to be important to us as helpers. We hired others. We had somebody come to model for us once a week. We began to get some portrait work. And then we were loading the canoe on the car again and heading for the woods.

We built a dam between two ridges to catch the run-off from melt and rainwater that made a creek at some seasons. Skeptics assured us that the fall rains would leave us just a ditch through the new dirt with a muddy cavity behind it. But the rushing water, with a little shovel guidance, found its way around the dam and over solid old land.

The trees have come crowding back around the pond; now they swarm over the dam itself. The pump that once sent water through pipes to many fenced fields is quiet. Fay has no trouble getting through the renascent brush that covers the road back, and I can still make it with a cane. If we stand there quietly for a while we are likely to see wild ducks come slanting down to splash into our little lake.

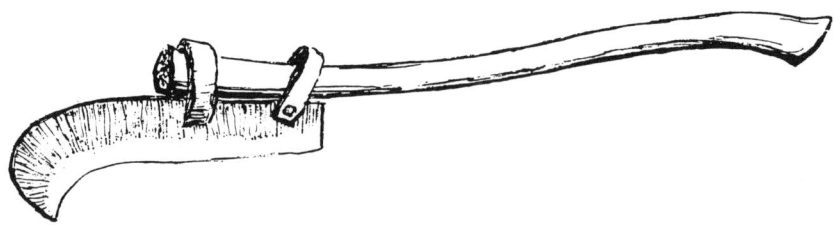

Chapter 16

PORTAGES

> The trail ran along a rock ridge, climbed
> a tree, and disappeared into a knot-hole.
>
> Nessmuk

"Hold it!"

Fay laid her paddle across the gunwales and pointed to something under the cedars. I pushed my blade down, angling it, braking against the water to check the canoe's forward glide.

"That black thing between the boulders," she said. "Yes, it's a

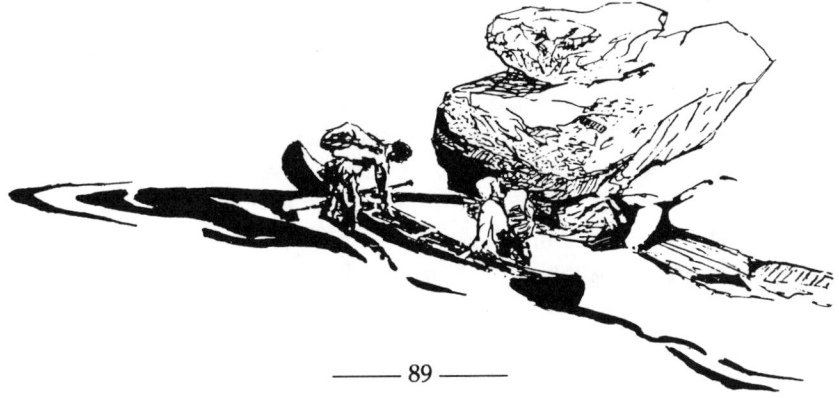

lard pail. Somebody's been cooking in it. And isn't that an opening in the brush behind it?"

"It must be a game trail. Canoes have been pulled up there all right and people have camped. But the portage wouldn't take off in that direction, nor up that hill. Look over there—that gap in the ridges. That's got to be the way to the next lake. And see what's opening up ahead of us. A nice bay that takes us right to it."

The battered black bucket was all but hollering.

"Wait," it was trying to tell us. "I'm a valuable implement. A little rusty but good for a lot of cooking yet. My Anishinabe family wouldn't throw me away. They left me because they'd be coming back here. Do you think they land this close to the end of the lake just for tea? Aren't you even going to look at that trail above me?"

Some of those vibrations must have gotten through. I looked back, trailed my paddle, missed a stroke. But I couldn't, or wouldn't, understand the kettle language. We pushed on into the inviting bay.

A stream entered from the direction of the break in the hills. We paddled up it until it shallowed, running over a stony bed. Here we got out and walked, dragging the lightened boat. We chopped through fallen timbers. Another creek came in, and from here on we had to take the packs on our backs and lift the canoe over the increasingly frequent spots where there wasn't enough depth to float it.

We were beginning to wish that we had taken the bucket's advice. By this time, though, we had invested so much time and sweat that it seemed best to push through whatever obstacles remained.

Late in the afternoon we were brought to a stop where what was left of our little river came spilling down the face of a cliff. There was nothing for it but to carry, drag, and paddle our way back to the pail trail. It gave us a steep climb, but nothing impossible. Once over the hump it rounded the waterfall and took us down to our lake. We had again been taught the lesson, emphasized by mild but memorable punishment: don't argue with the portage.

On the well-tended canoe routes of parks and national forests you don't usually have to ponder such decisions. As you approach a portage you may see a sign giving the name of the next lake or stream and the distance to it. Often there will be a log dock for your convenience. At least you'll be able to count on a conspicuous blaze, an axe-scar on a tree facing the water where a well-worn path leads on.

Such trails are kept clear of brush and fallen timber. At grateful intervals you are likely to find horizontal poles nailed to trees, where you can lean your canoe while you step out from under it to rest your shoulders. Best of all, these refined portages will never endanger your life and limb, or ask you to attempt some desperate effort.

But if you go north beyond the officially protected places you will soon be walking over a different kind of portage. It may take you over a log across a distressingly deep and rocky gully. Or up a slope so steep that, tilting your head back, you wonder how anybody ever got a canoe up there. One man may have to climb with a line attached to the bow, and then hoist while the other gets under the canoe and struggles up with it.

Land and water trails may shade into each other. You carry your boat down a softening path, your feet sinking deeper into the ooze at each step. The portage gradually becomes a slough. Maybe you can frog it through: set the canoe down in a pool and drag it, swimming through the deep holes, or give it a shove and trail yourself out behind it to the next foothold. In this kind of going you don't get into the boat any oftener than you have to because every time you do you drip off a bucket of liquid mud into it.

When streams are blocked by fallen timber you squeeze under or drag over if you can, but some of the trees may have to be axed out. Chopping them from a floating canoe is frustrating work. A chain saw would do it easily, but you don't carry such heavy hardware on this kind of a trip.

The ancient routes, bad as they often seem, are always the best way through. They were established, tested, altered, and corrected down over the centuries by men and women on their ways to hunt, trap, or fish, to harvest rice or sugar, to make war on their enemies or to escape from them—all life-and-death necessities in an evenly balanced struggle for survival.

These people weren't just taking fun trips. They *had* to get from this body of water to that one. They would always take the shortest, safest, and easiest path. If there was no short, safe, or easy path, they would take the least bad way.

Canoeists who have strayed away from the officially approved route may react to the first of these punishing portages with outrage. "What's the matter with the management? Do they expect us to go there?"

No, up here nobody but you cares where you go. You can find yourself a detour if you like. But be sure that if you search for a week you won't find a better way.

For a white man, it may be impossible to follow the trail. Oh, not impossible, because what one man can do, another can do too, regardless of race. Present-day canoeists are not being driven across it by famine or chased by the Sioux. If it looks too tough to you, you can turn around and go home. The old ones had to get through or die.

There are no printed signs to mark the landings. A dim grown-over blaze, maybe. There may be no visible marking, so that you have to make your guess from the lay of the land. You ease your canoe along close to the shore, looking sharp for the trace that must take off here somewhere.

Some of the old trails are hard to find now and growing more so. Others are kept open, after a fashion, by deer, bear, and moose. This may be for only part of the way. When the animals get as far as they want to go on the path, they just take off into the woods. The brush grows in beyond.

I was walking along such a dying trail with the canoe on my shoulders, shoving it against more and more aggressively encroaching branches until I had to admit that I was no place except just in the deep woods. I stood the boat on its stern with the bow wedged into a vee of birches, and walked back, marking my path by breaking twigs to show the light under-sides of the leaves. I didn't want to lose the trail and the canoe both.

Working this way I came out on a ridge where stone of the old portage still showed, a straight line worn down through the moss by many moccasins. With this for a start and not bent under a load, I was able to follow the traces of the faded path to the river.

Such country provides plenty of incentive for going light. Before each trip I used to revise my list of equipment and supplies, crossing out items that didn't seem essential, and substituting lighter or less bulky necessities.

Fay not only put up with this diminishing outfit but took an active interest in cutting it down further. She kept notes on a page in her sketchbook of what might be left at home next time.

In earlier years I would give a guest a list of what he might take. Before starting I would inspect his pack, stripping it of unauthorized comforts.

He might plead, "This weighs so little," or "I'll carry this in my pocket." Then I would patiently but firmly explain that littles add up to lots and that unnecessary weights are worse on the person than in the pack. The best place to carry burdens is on your back, not stuffed into pockets.

Canned food was taboo. No use carrying water when there's so much of it out there. So we favored dry stuff like flour, rice, beans, oatmeal, prunes, dried apples. Sliced bacon mildews in wet weather, but an uncut slab in a cloth sack holds up well. You get to like those thick strips knifed off it. Some luxuries such as nuts and chocolate pay their way in calories.

For this kind of travel you want plenty of calories per pound. You don't have to worry about getting fat on a canoe trip. You'll put on pounds if you're underweight or take them off if you're too heavy.

One cooking kettle with no plates is enough if you're with a consenting adult. You take it off the fire, set it between you, and eat out of it together like desert Arabs or the Hebrew patriarchs. It's a nice gesture, intimate in a scriptural way, and saves weight and dish washing.

But don't try it with small kids. Their flying spoons will empty the pan before the grown-ups are well started.

We marked boundaries in the porridge. The children would eat swiftly up to the line and then wait, with spoons poised. When our portion crumbled into their territory it would be instantly gobbled. We went back to one private tin plate for each person.

I never could see any need for swimming suits in these comparatively untraveled waters. But it's all right to have woolen underwear even in summer for cool nights or the streak of cold, rainy weather that may happen at any time of the year.

Toilet paper is a bulky luxury, usually soggy and obviously unnecessary in a country where leaves and moss are everywhere in summer and where dry sticks are always at hand in winter. My traveling granddaughter, Kris, tells me that most people in Asia and Africa wouldn't know what toilet paper was for if they saw it. And yet I have caught more than one otherwise honest person trying to sneak some of it along in his pack or pocket.

Speaking of moss, it's also useful in cleaning greasy pans. You can do the job even with cold water, dirt side first and then mossy side.

Summer nights are short in the North. If you start early in the morning you'll be camped and finished with the chores before dark, so that you won't need any artificial light.

For other seasons, a palouse weighs less and lasts longer than a flashlight. This is a tin can with a wire handle attached to its upper side and a candle pushed up through an x-shaped slash in the under side. It throws a strong light, doesn't blow out easily in the wind, and you don't have to be stingy about using it the way you do with batteries. But you must remember to push the candle higher from time to time or it will drop out burning.

We made our packs in the Anishinabe fashion, piling the contents on a canvas spread on the ground. We'd wrap and bind this into a bundle, to which we'd tie a tump line.

The tump line! That ancient thing of beauty and of sweat-stained efficiency! Down through the years it has been used to move enormous burdens over the trails of the North American wilderness.

In keeping with the universal principles of art, the loveliness of the tumpline begins with utter simplicity. A broad strap of heavy leather narrows to end in thongs that can be tied around any bundle, bale or box. The widest part of the strap goes over the top of the head, not across the forehead as in the movies.

Once the load is hanging from the head and resting against the hips, other articles are piled upon it until the burden reaches the capacity of the bearer. Then off he goes, or, more often, she, while the man carries the canoe. She trots along at a quick clip where the footing is good. The faster the pace, the sooner the load will be off her back.

If danger threatens—danger from man, beast, bog, breaking ice or a slippery pole over a gully—the load can be dumped instantly with a toss of the head. So it's a good way to move cargo. But vision is limited to a few feet of the trail directly ahead.

In early years I often went alone and on foot. This called for a more drastic reduction of food and furniture than any water-born journey.

The Poirers made me a little silk tarp that weighed less than a pound. It could always be tied to trees, snags, or bushes, one way or another depending on the wind, to give as much shelter as I needed. I also took a pack sack, jackknife, map, compass, matches, blanket, .22 rifle, a piece of fish line and a few hooks.

I made my bed by scraping out hollows in the dirt for hips and shoulders. Over these I'd lay the empty pack sack, with the flap spread out to keep the damp from my body. On a summer night I would bend a green twig and stick both ends into the ground to make an arch over my head, then drape a piece of mosquito netting on it, and tuck it in to cover my face.

Having no axe, I made the fire Indian-fashion with sticks laid out like the spokes of a wheel. As they burned away I would push them in towards the hub. For bannock I poured a little water into a hollow in the top of a sack of biscuit mix, stirred it right there in the bag, then wrapped the dough around a green stick and baked it by the fire. There are several ways to cook meat and fish without a pan, but the easiest is to roast it on a green forked stick, with a smaller stick skewered in as needed to keep a flat surface to the fire. Berries you pick and eat where they grow.

I had my waterproof shelter for sleeping, but when it rained during the day I just got wet. That was all right if I kept moving. I drank on hands and knees, lifting my head to let the water run down my throat.

Making camp was quick and easy. No poles nor balsam bedding to cut and haul in, no water to carry, no dishes to wash.

All camping carries the appeal of a return to an ancestral past, but going without gadgets takes you furthest back into the primitive. Like so many good things, though, it is for the young. I wouldn't be able to live through it now.

Chapter 17

THE FEMALE OF THE SPECIES

> When the Himalayan peasant meets the he-bear in his pride
> He shouts to scare the monster, who will often turn aside
> But the she-bear, thus accosted, rends the peasant tooth
>   and nail
> For the female of the species is more deadly than the male.
>   Kipling

Schplat!

    The racket of branches beating on the inverted hull couldn't quite kill that sound. A big foot had schplatted down into a puddle in the portage trail just behind me. I twisted around, tilted up the side of the canoe, and peered back from under the gunwale into the long face of a cow moose. She had stopped short to keep from bumping the boat. A calf poked his head out from behind her inquiringly. "What's the trouble, ma? What's holding us up?"

    A bull moose that close might have been pawing the ground, whacking the brush with his antlers, and making little bluffs at a charge. And I would have been up a tree because I wouldn't be quite sure that they were bluffs.

But I didn't feel any menace in the cow's silent stare. I went on down the trail, listening to the footsteps just behind me. When I set the canoe down in the water and turned back, my two followers had disappeared.

She hadn't been one of those deadly females. She had just been keeping an eye on me while I crossed her territory. I might not have led that parade so calmly if the incident had been preceded by one that happened the following summer.

Roe and I unloaded on the moss-covered dock of a deserted logging camp. He started up the trail with the canoe. I poked some loose items into a pack, swung it to my back, and set a smaller pack above it. That made a good load.

I had followed the old tote road for about half a mile when I heard a snort ahead. A whitetail doe was standing in the trail, stiff-legged and alert.

I stopped, wished for Roe and his camera, then plodded on, expecting her to fade into the brush.

Instead she came toward me.

I had been told that a doe could split a wolf's skull if she could catch him with her hooves. I had never heard of one attacking a man.

That seemed to be her idea now. Her ears were laid back, her eyes were rolling wildly, and the hair on the back of her neck was standing up like a broom. She zoomed up on hind legs, growing suddenly big.

I jerked my head back. The tump strap slipped off backwards and the packs thudded to the ground. I jumped aside. Her front hooves struck down on a pack. One leg caught for a moment in the strap.

The second growth aspens along the trail were too thin and whippy to be climbed. A dead spruce lay beside me. I grabbed it up, swinging its top to meet her next attack, the butt still on the ground. She was on her hind feet again, but the bristling branches of the tree kept her from getting at me with her front hooves.

She bounded off on all fours, then came back from one side, weaving in like a boxer. I swung the spruce to meet her. She moved back, unwilling to plunge against the stiff curve of the branches.

She shifted, seeming to look for an opening. While she hesitated, a little spotted fawn ran out to her. She looked down at it, up at me, then led it off into the woods.

I stepped cautiously out into the trail. In a flash she was back. I jumped behind my tree for another *pas de deux*. She disappeared again as Roe came around a bend in the trail. We picked up the packs and went on.

From time to time I looked back. Then there she was again. Just following now, though, not closing in. She stayed with us until we paddled away from the portage.

Before we left it, Roe took a photo of her. That, of course, is just a picture of a deer, not a proof of my strange story. Not to anybody else. But when I look at it the whole affair comes back to me and I know that it's not just a senile wandering of memory.

☙❧

A bank job in the thirties carried certain occupational hazards. At a time when most people were underpaid, unemployed, or losing money, a few talented and imaginative bank-robbers had made their calling look not only profitable, but also glamorous and heroic.

The public has always disliked bankers, and with good reason. Ever since the middle ages they have despised us for our sin of usury. We keep people from doing what they want to do and make them pay debts that they don't want to pay. They watch us carry grandma out of the foreclosed house in her chair and set her down on the sidewalk, still rocking. Sometimes they used to put us in jail or do worse than that to us. But they can't get along without us either.

Naturally, bankers were the villains of the depression. Men and women were taking up the bandit profession all over the United States and were not meeting with unanimous public disapproval. Some of the action was uncomfortably close to home.

An aunt and uncle of mine were dragged from their bed in a Wisconsin country town. The robbers left Aunt Mame bound and gagged in the house, while they escorted Uncle Baxter to his small bank. When he was unable to remember the combination of the safe they opened the draft of the coal stove and pushed a poker into it. As the iron took on a nice cherry red, my uncle found that he could remember the required numbers. His visitors put the money into a sack and left, remarking that they were glad not to have had to apply the poker.

Not everybody got off that easily. While two of our Proctor tellers, followed by an armed guard, were carrying the railroad payday money from the depot to the bank, a car pulled up beside them. There was a blast of gunfire and the guard fell dead. The other men dropped their bundles and ran, speeded by more shots, but not hit.

That happened during the winter while I was at college. When I came back to work in June the tellers' cages had been converted into a fortress with steel plate, bullet proof glass, and gun ports. On railroad paydays we would be stationed along the block between the depot and the bank, our hands on sketchily concealed revolvers, our eyes on every stranger or unfamiliar automobile. The new guard was armed with a sawed-off pump gun. It sounds like wild west stuff now, but it was all part of a banker's job in those days.

I never got to shoot anybody, but Fay almost did.

After the Lindbergh kidnapping, with its deliberate murder and big ransom payment, some bank robbers began using similar tactics. They went for wives and children instead of the vault. This was not a new idea in itself, but now there had developed a nasty tendency first to kill the hostage and then demand the payment. Family banks seemed particularly vulnerable.

Fay and I kept our guns loaded with buckshot. It was agreed that if anyone broke into the house we would shoot him without parley.

One night when I was out of town, Fay was alone with our two-year-old son. Towards midnight she was waked by furtive sounds from the front porch. She had locked the door there herself, and also the side door, but the "girl" had left later through the kitchen. Esther had several times forgotten to lock that door on her way out.

Fay was six months pregnant. She sat down quietly at the head of the stairs, with her shotgun on her knees, ready to take steady aim at anybody coming up.

She heard the intruder try the side door and then go around to the back. There was the sound of the vestibule door opening. Sure enough, Esther had forgotten to lock it.

The handle of the inner door clicked one way and then the other. It was locked. But just with an indoor lock that could be forced with a strong kick, or opened with any old skeleton key.

The visitor shook the door angrily, then drove his shoulder against it. Hard, but not hard enough to break through.

Fay heard him leave through the vestibule and close the outer door. She called the police. They didn't find the man, but said that somebody had been snooping around other houses in the neighborhood. That guy never knew how lucky he was.

At about this time, J. Edgar Hoover was reorganizing the FBI. When they had killed off a few of the most illustrious Robin Hoods, the crime wave subsided. Hoover and his organization have had a lot of bad press, but they looked good to us. It was a comfort to have the names of those celebrated killers on headstones instead of in headlines.

Later, on the farm, Fay looked out the window just at the moment when the leghorn rooster, having tipped over our three-year-old daughter, was trying to drive his spurs into her head. Fay took off, looking for a weapon as she accelerated. She snatched a broom from beside the door, swung it back as she came across the yard, and aimed a fierce blow. The rooster jumped out of her way and made his escape. In spite of his concentration on Beryl he had seen the approaching fury. Another lucky guy. Fay told me later that she would have attacked an elephant.

At this point she lost interest in the guilty chicken and turned to see what damage had been done. It was a cool day and Beryl had been wearing a hooded jacket that gave her considerable protection. She was bleeding a little, but not crying. The raid and the rescue had all happened so fast that she hadn't had time to get scared.

The moral of these last two stories is that a sweet, gentle woman may become a deadly danger to man or bird. When her child is threatened, even a concert pianist can turn into something with a broomstick.

Males and male-dominated institutions, including nations, may fight to the death because of a noble, unreasoning determination to conquer the adversary. Let's call this kind of courage rooster valor.

While the last breaths sag out of you, you stagger somehow to your feet, stab your spur into your crowing enemy, and die happy while he flops in bloody plumage on the floor beside you.

We are a grand old sex. Females are disgracefully lacking in rooster valor.

A little cur rushed, yipping wildly, at our competent old cat. She scooted up a tree and smiled down at him from the branches. I was ashamed of her. I thought that one swipe from her claws would have sent him flying.

But when a big, black, mean-looking police dog got close to her kittens, she jumped at him. The last I saw of him she was riding him down the road like a jockey on a race horse. Except that she kept reaching forward trying to get at his eyes.

Any dog that knows how to handle cats could have broken her back with one shake. Not being sure, I suppose, which one might be so skilled, she made a policy of giving them all plenty of room. But she didn't hesitate to take her chances with the big one when she judged that the kittens were in danger.

Out in the back forty one morning, I found a turkey dead under a roosting tree—dead and half-eaten, with feathers scattered about. I knew that whoever had done it would be back for more. So that evening I returned, carrying a shotgun.

The trail passes through a low area, with alders twisting up above open pools bordered with cowslips. Here a little owl, the size of my fist, swung silently down around my head, flew away, then returned for a closer pass. The next time back she really came for me. I warded her off with the gun barrel. She tried again, skimming in from behind, and dug her claws into my hair.

This was long and shaggy enough so that she did me no damage. Still, such single-minded intensity of purpose was beginning to bother me. It would have been ridiculous to shoot such a tiny thing in self defense, but on her next swoop I hit her a pretty good belt with the gun barrel.

That seemed to knock some sense into her. She swung low another time or two, but didn't attack again.

I suppose I'd passed near her nest.

We didn't willingly share our turkeys with the varmints, but it was worth some apples to watch the deer and bear.

One bear came each afternoon with her two cubs up the little hill below the house. Fay watched them through the window. Once,

when the mother was just about to take the first bite from branches bent down with fruit, she stopped. She stood there a moment, then rose on her hind legs, looking down into the woods. Then she dropped back on all fours and hurried the youngsters out of the clearing in the opposite direction. None of them had even tasted an apple.

As they left, a big male ambled out of the brush and up the grade. He ate all he wanted and left. Immediately a smaller male came out for his share. The mother and cubs didn't show up again until next day. Like the cat, she wasn't taking any chances.

At the beginning of his career as a meat producer, a male piglet has to be castrated. Otherwise he would just grow up into a stringy, crabby boar.

The hardest part of the operation, for me, was separating the little animal from its ma. Some sows don't pay much attention, but others object violently.

Real hog growers in real farming country, of course, must have a safe and convenient method. But in my bulletin, the Department of Agriculture confined itself to the surgical procedure.

The only way that I could think of was to hang around looking innocent until the old lady was at the other end of the yard. Then grab the victim and over the fence like John, John, the piper's son.

This action fascinated Mike, our German shepherd. He was forbidden to enter the pig yard. But on these occasions he hung around it, watching with repressed excitement.

One rainy day I was making my snatch. This little pig squealed, and instantly his mother started for us at a speed amazing for her bulk.

That was all part of the usual act, but this time there was a slip. Sprinting for the fence with the loud piglet under my arm, I hit a slick spot. My feet shot out ahead and I came down hard. I rolled over, trying to get up. My hands slipped in the mud and manure. A dark, avenging shape loomed over me. The speeding sow had arrived.

She had arrived, but she continued to loom. Her charge had halted. Snorting, she swung away from me. I scrambled to my feet and over the fence.

Looking back I saw a swirling cartwheel of hog and dog. Mike had jumped in and grabbed her by the hock. When he saw that I was in the clear he let go and got out of there.

You probably know how a dog looks when he's done something really wicked. That hangdog expression. Mike looked as guilty as sin. He had violated the sanctity of the pigpen.

I made use of maternal ferocity in the studio. When a girl got up on the model stand for the first time she was likely to feel hopelessly self-conscious. So I devised a bit of play-acting that was usually effective in loosening up a stiff little novice.

"You are a primitive mother. Your baby is lying there on the floor of the cave. A saber-tooth tiger is reaching out a paw to grab him.

"You have just this one chance to harpoon the tiger. Now swing this spear back"—I handed her an aluminum pole—"and call up all the strength you have to stab it into him."

It is a part that could be acted instantly by any woman. The nudity and unfamiliar surroundings were forgotten. She would drop back her right foot to brace herself, twist her torso, and take aim at the marauder. My charcoal would jab and slide over the paper. We were a working team. The next pose would come naturally.

One of the girls said, "I would have rammed it right through that old tiger!"

Chapter 18

A WINTER'S TALE

> When the snowflakes, whirling downward,
> Hissed among the withered oak leaves.
> Changed the pine trees into wigwams,
> Covered all the earth with silence....
> Longfellow

The snowflakes had been whirling downward all night, bending branches into hollow cones around each spruce to make wigwams for the wabooz, the long-legged, splay-footed white hares. The earth was covered with silence.

Fay and I had started early that morning, allowing what we thought would be plenty of time to reach the old cabin at Seven Beaver Lake.

The weather stayed warm and the snow continued. The snowshoes sank deep into the soft white, and a burden of snow fell in at each step to be hoisted on the uplift. Moloch, the big, hay-colored Chesapeake retriever, out of his element here, floundered behind. Heavy going for all three of us.

Late in the afternoon the snow stopped. The sun broke briefly through the clouds, casting a warm light over the trail, then disappeared behind the trees. A timber wolf called and was answered by another. The air turned cold. Later we learned that the temperature had dropped to forty below that night. But you didn't need a thermometer to know that it was cold.

The path petered out. We followed winding rabbit roads. It was getting too dark to read the compass. We hadn't planned to camp out and had no tent. It was becoming clear that we were not going to make it to the cabin that night.

"Looks like we'll have to siwash it."

"What's that?"

"Bivouac in the snow."

Fay didn't say anything, but I knew what she was thinking. This would be her first experience in winter camping.

As night comes on, in this kind of cold, a person becomes aware that he is where he doesn't belong. It's like diving way down into deep water where light gives way to darkness and your eardrums bend in under the pressure. You know that you won't stay alive very long unless you do something different.

With the snowshoes we shoveled down to the moss in a spruce thicket. We propped poles against one tree and covered them with boughs cut from others. We brought in a lot of firewood.

Fay set boughs in place to make a bed. I broke open an old pine stump and started a fire with the pitchy wood. When it lighted up our shelter the menace of the winter wilderness gave way, as it always does, to the comfortable feeling of warmth and safety.

We slept well most of the night. Only once in a while the fire would die down and the cold nudge me a little. Then I would push the blackened sticks and lumps together and blow on them until they first glowed and then flamed. I put on more wood and went back to sleep.

While we had been out gathering that wood we had seen a timber wolf, a shadowy shape that slid across an opening in a clump of cedars. We had heard more singing. Moloch heard too and kept close to the fire.

If those had been literary wolves, familiar with Jack London and Little Red Riding Hood, they would undoubtedly have made use of the burned-out intervals to come in and eat us. There would have been nothing left but two belt buckles and one collar buckle.

But these were ignorant backwoods wolves with no appetite for people. Just interested. I don't know about Moloch, though, if he'd wandered out amongst them. He didn't.

In the morning they were gone, leaving only tracks in the snow.

We packed up, tied on our snowshoes, and shuffled into the woods. Good walking now on the frozen crust. We came out on the lake and crossed it to our cabin. Ours in the sense that it was our destination. Chink and I had slept in it several times without finding out who owned it.

In those days cabins weren't locked. In any one of them we could usually count on finding a battered axe, a bucket, a fry pan, a couple of musty blankets, and a can of bacon grease. The grease was always sprinkled with mouse droppings, but those could be scraped off. It tasted wonderful in a hungry emergency.

Woods people had their faults, but they didn't ordinarily go in for stealing. The constant threat of starvation demanded that when food, ammunition, or other supplies were left in a cache or cabin they would be there when the owner came back for them. That was the Indian tradition. It was followed by almost all white woodsmen.

Anybody leaving a cabin made sure that there would be wood in it for the next person. Fay got some of this burning in the stove, then went into the forest for more. I walked out on the frozen lake with the axe and pail.

The December ice was thick and it took some chopping. After a while I was leaning down over a deep hole, splashing at every stroke as the water came up after the first break-through. When the open

ing was big enough I pushed the bucket down through it and pulled it up full.

When I got back to the cabin I needed some de-icing myself. But it beats setting a pan of snow on the stove. That melts down to near nothing and never tastes like real water.

A winter night is so long that you can't sleep it all away. So you need an artificial light. We heated the can of bacon grease and dipped a rag in it several times, letting it cool between dippings. It made a smelly, sputtering candle, not much as a reading light, but usable.

The next day I went hunting. As an experiment in saving weight I had brought the little .22 cartridges known as shorts instead of the usual long-rifles.

A grouse was eating buds in the top branches of a tall aspen. I took careful aim, fired, and saw feathers fly. The partridge jerked, stretched its neck, looked all around, and went back to feeding. I took several more shots, missing some and getting no better results with those that hit. The puny little slugs were slapping so lightly at that height that the bird didn't even know that he was being attacked.

There were other grouse at lower levels. We plucked them while they were still warm and roasted them on sticks thrust down into the stove, with the lid put back as nearly in place as possible to keep us from being smoked out.

We stayed in the cabin for several days. Before we left we swept the floor and brought in wood. The can had already been refilled for mice or men with our own surplus bacon grease.

We didn't always find such luxurious quarters, but there is plenty of fuel in the forest. We could get comfortable with our open tent and a fire. In later years, when arthritis had begun to assert itself, I felt the need of more shelter. We tried a strip of canvas, supported by poles, running from the opening of the tent around the fire and back to the other side of the opening. That kept us warm but we had to be careful not to let the flame get close to the cloth. Kris and I had to jump out of our blankets one night, dump water on the blazing canvas, and beat out what still smoldered.

More effective but less portable was a sheet of corrugated aluminum curved into a half-teepee, with smoke-hole at the top, to stand over the fire and reflect the heat into the tent. We tied the canvas door flaps to poles set close to the metal but not touching it.

With this combination and a chain saw I had real comfort no matter how deep the temperature dived. I felt that if I had my choice I'd stay right here in the woods for the rest of my life. But the aluminum, although light, was too floppy to carry far. With the saw, it pretty well limited us to places where we could drive.

People who can get along without such luxuries are free to travel where they please over frozen waterways and snowy portage trails. That means going light, but adequate food, clothes and bedding still make a load. Lacking dogs, I'd rather carry them on my back than on a toboggan, which can be heavy pulling in fresh snow. Snowshoes beat skis when a pack is to be carried through brush or over rough ground.

Snow machines—motorized toboggans—are fast if the route is easy, flat, and open. Like the outboard motor they have had an en-

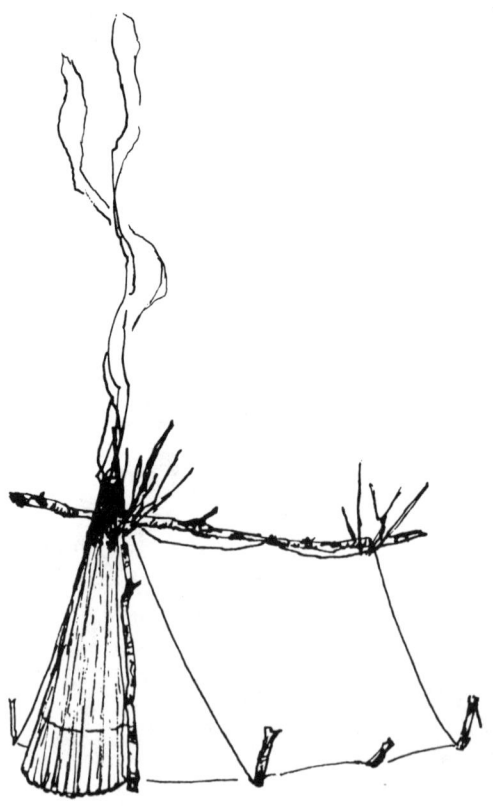

thusiastic reception from people, white and brown, who live in the woods. Also like the outboard and the gasoline saw, they aren't much good when they get beyond the big lakes and flat rivers that connect with roads. They are frustrating on overgrown trails or in cross-country runs through rough or brushy terrain. They can't carry enough gasoline to go very far. For a long trip in the wilderness or arctic they have to be supplied by air. They destroy fragile vegetation by packing down snow and ice over it.

Snow machines are involved in many accidents with a disturbing percentage of fatalities. They crash into snow-hidden rocks, break through ice that would support a toboggan and dog team, and show a weird weakness for mechanical failure in remote places. Experienced snowmobilers make it a rule to carry snowshoes and light camping equipment, but there isn't room for much of that unless a sled is in tow.

Whenever I've gone any place on a snow machine I've been delighted and a little surprised to get off it alive. The great popularity that they enjoyed was probably due less to their merit than to their status as winter acolytes of the gadget god. It comes as a relief to note that they are not nearly so widely used now as they were a few years ago.

As the years and the bone joints have tightened on me, I have become addicted to the four-wheel drive truck, almost as unholy as the snow machine although not so noisy or suicidal. Still, I've lobbied for legislation to keep them both out of wilderness areas. So at least I'm not one of those old goofers who demand that conservation rules be relaxed to allow them to continue our depredations beyond their normal span.

Therefore let us rejoice while we are young.

With snowshoes and a pack you can go where you please in the winter forest. Wind can't keep you off the water now. Swamps and gullies won't impede you on the trails. The mosquito minstrels of summer are quiet.

And not just the mosquitoes. The snow has covered all the earth with silence. You can let down the guard that you didn't know you'd erected against the unrelenting racket of civilization.

The few sounds that do reach you are welcome. In this quiet they may come from far away: the hammering of a woodpecker, the crunch and squeak of distant snowshoes, the calls of an assembling wolf pack. Or at night, as you doze off in the fire warmth, the sounds of the deepening cold: the crack of frost in a tree or the ice-roar from a tightening lake.

Chapter 19

INSECTS IN THE IMPASTO

Aesthetics is for the artists as ornithology is for the birds.
Barnett Newman

The cliffs of Pie Island rose straight and tall. Taller than the walls of a giant's castle. Their squared towers and parapets glowed red in the sunset. Eight hundred feet below, waves broke against their base, dark in the endless shadow of the mainland hills. Big swells of water, no longer whipped on by 'Tschgumi's winds, rolled listlessly, like tired fighters that strike without fury.

All afternoon Fay and I had been waiting for this easing. Now it was time to come out of hiding and cross the traverse.

Later, as we neared the island, cold now in moonlight, its name seemed singularly commonplace for such a magnificent mass of stone. But we could see how its shape had reminded the voyageurs of a French pâté.

We were steering for the place where a slice had been cut out of the pie. The break seemed to indicate a possible point of entry, a low spot where a river from one of the lakes in the interior had breached the wall.

We landed on a beach of rounded rocks and camped on the narrow strip of earth above it. By this time the moon had gone down, but we could hear the stream not far away in the quiet dark.

Next morning we climbed the trail beside it and came into a clearing where a cabin, in the process of being taken over by the returning forest, was in a lovely state of dilapidation. A stove pipe, crooked and red with rust, still stood above the sagging curve of the roof. Through ragged holes in the curtain of spruce behind it, we could see the deep blue of Lake Superior.

When a painter comes on such a scene he feels that something has to be done about it. We set up our easels in the shade. I squeezed out big gobs of oil and went to work with a palette knife.

This has a long, flexible blade with a rounded point. It's not the kind of a knife you'd want to have in a bear-fight, but it's just the thing for spreading a layer of paint quickly and reasonably evenly. You swing it from the shoulder and follow through as though it were a tennis racket.

I like to trowel one smear of the colored grease over another while the whole thing is still wet. You never know just what's going to happen. The coat beneath may stay obediently submerged, or it may break through in spots, or it may mix with the top layer. The unexpected results often turn out better than anything I could have planned. It is as loose a technique as any watercolor and depends as much on random chance and lucky accident. Then it has such a nice Italian name: *impasto*.

I had been reading a book about how to get along with flies and mosquitoes. The writer makes a good case for peaceful co-existence. He keeps his thoughts friendly. "We're all brothers and sisters in this hard world. I wouldn't think of doing you any harm. And I'm sure that you'll eat only a reasonable amount of me."

He claimed that primitive people have this accord with nature. He cited the Indians as an example.

The Indians I know now are no more bug-proof than I am, but then they're no more primitive either. I can remember marveling, in earlier years, at how the woods Indians survived without dope or netting. Maybe they did have an understanding with the biters, suckers, and stingers.

The islands in this part of Lake Superior are always cool at night, but they can get hot under the summer sun. The air was muggy that morning, and I was working without a shirt. I don't like the smell or feel of insect repellent, and in that kind of weather you sweat it right off anyway. So I was dopeless as well as shirtless. It seemed a good opportunity to try out the philosophical approach.

For a while it did seem to work. I was being crawled all over but not chawed much.

Maybe they were just looking over the field before starting work. Maybe everything would have come out just as the book said if I had kept my part of the bargain. I'll never know.

I began to resent all those friendly little feet tramping up and down my spine, and to object to even the moderate nibbling that was going on. My mind was trying to concentrate on the painting, neglecting mental welcomes. At the same time evil feelings were sprouting in my subconscious.

I made a small, absent-minded, or at least unpremeditated, swat. I doubt that it hurt anybody. But the change in the tempo of the buzzing made it clear that the bugs were shocked at this betrayal of confidence. Retaliation was swift. Soon I was slapping and they were buzzing and biting just like always.

So this is one of several unfinished experiments that I hand down, in this book, for more dedicated people to carry further.

The painting was coming pretty well, as paintings often do when circumstance is clutching at the artist, distracting him from too much smoothing and correcting. I was so excited that I continued to trowel on the impasto and bat bugs all morning and well into the afternoon.

There were deer flies in the crowd, and when I finished I was well smeared with blood and paint. Some of the little brothers and one or two that were quite big had been plastered into the painting. Later, back in the studio, I literally worked the bugs out of it.

I was pleased with this finished painting. It sold promptly, so somebody else liked it too. But it wasn't the kind of picture that would have won me a pat on the head from the art experts.

A long time before this I had reached the conclusion that I would never gain the approval of those authorities without making some radical changes. Changes not only in painting but also in principles.

Freud said that the artist's goals are fame, riches, and the love of beautiful women. Maybe some guys can reach out with their paintbrushes and latch on to those last two highly desirable items. If so, I take off my hat to them, because I can think of easier ways.

As to fame, well, it may be an aim for the kids. I didn't have to be in the business very long to get that inspiration out my mind.

After eighty years of on-and-off painting I will have to admit that there is still a lot I don't know about it. But one thing I have learned for sure: this year's great art will be next year's trash. So if it's fame you're after, enjoy it while it lasts.

In the twenties, when I was becoming aware of such matters, fauvism and cubism were already old fashioned. They were being supplanted in "discriminating collections" by dadaism and other recent imports. These crashed with the stock market in 1929, and everybody rushed into New Deal social consciousness: big working men and their amazonian women bravely upsetting and dumping spatted Republican oppressors. Within a few years, though, even these formidable people were overthrown in favor of abstract expressionism.

It would be unkind as well as useless to list here all the theories, styles, schools, circles, and salons that have, since that time, had their moments of supremacy. The priests and devotees of each of them have spoken contemptuously of its predecessor. Each movement has been copiously imitated by artists and art students, urged on by the insistent demands of critics, galleries, teachers, and collectors. Each has been cast down and verbally spat upon by the same shamans who had set it up as an object of worship.

Now it's all very proper to defy art lords who demand that I paint the way they tell me to paint. But I'd better not scorn all the work that has, for a time, won their flitting favor. Because, of course, fine work has been done in each of these fashions and each has been used by others who came later. I might not have dared to trowel down those layers of bug-paint mixture if I hadn't been loosened up by the abstractionists.

Since the non-representational movement we have seen the opposite extreme. If the model doesn't have a mole in some prominent location the photo-realist will put one in to make his picture photo-real. Wildlife and western artists have always delighted their patrons by including even the most insignificant detail. Lately they have been making a good enough thing out of it that they can put up with being called "just illustrators, not artists."

I like money, but when I've tried their technique, tickling in every leaf and feather, my trees and creatures have gone lifeless. I prefer to follow Napoleon's maxim. Take plenty of time to plan the overall strategy, but carry out the actual tactics with élan. Stare for as long as you please at the paper or canvas. Doodle and diagram and sketch. But when it's time to put on paint, slam out the brushwork with speed and excitement, as well as with excruciating effort.

You are, of course, viewing with suspicion these comments about my own work or that of my contemporaries. We are the mothers, not the fathers, of our pictures. We don't just beget them in some pleasant, casual moment. We give birth to them in pain and travail. They are always noble and beautiful in our eyes, even those that look like nasty brats to the rest of the world.

But that other guy's paintings . . . .

When Nell Gwynne, woman of the world and mistress of Charles II, was publicly snubbed at the king's ball by the top duchess, she remarked sweetly, understandingly, and very audibly, "Folk love not others in the same trade."

That is especially true of art. We are fiercely jealous of others in our trade. We sawed almost through the supports of the Sistine scaffold in the hope that Michelangelo would break his damned neck. So you are quite right in discounting any nasty remarks that one painter makes about the work of others.

Art is an addiction and art teachers ought to be dealt with like drug pushers. I have been blessed with a feeble conscience and have had no qualms about introducing young people to drawing and painting. But the worst scoundrel has to draw the line somewhere. I never told any of them that they'd make money at it.

Once a person gets the habit he goes right on turning out pictures regardless of whether they are good or bad, salable or unsalable—which is by no means the same: a good picture may be unsalable or the other way round.

He can always ask himself, who knows what is great art? If, as usually happens, nobody wants his paintings at any price, he piles them for posterity in the attic, basement, or woodshed.

Fay and I came up against the art surplus disposal problem during our early years on the farm. We were painting oils on hardboard because it was cheaper than canvas. It also happens to be a better ground, especially if you are working with heavy paint. We were producing a lot of pictures, selling very few, and it was time to make room for next winter's wood in the woodshed.

One day we stacked a lot of oil paintings on a brush pile and set fire to it. The pile had stood for a while, but it was too green for this job. It burned, but not hotly enough to do away with the hardboard. Here we found watercolors and pastels definitely superior to oils. Being painted on paper, they burned beautifully.

After further experiments we found a way to take care of the oils too. They made excellent garden mulch. We laid them between the rows of young plants, where they moldered slowly, preventing weed growth and keeping the soil moist.

I consider this discovery my greatest achievement in art. I am happy to be able to contribute it here. I haven't seen it written up in any of the art publications.

This is strange, because it is a problem that artists have always had to face. Oils have been reverently removed, after the painter's death has given them value, from the roofs of outhouses, where they had been used to patch holes. At least one of Rembrandt's big paintings, done during that period of unpopularity in his late life when he was producing his best work, was sold by its owner for scrap canvas. Tom Thomson, greatest of the Canadian Group of Seven, painted landscapes on pieces of slab wood that he picked up from the throwaway pile at the lumber mill, so that he could use them in the winter to heat his shack. Van Gogh sold just one picture during his lifetime, and that was to his brother. His sister-in-law stuffed the attic with the discards, and they made her children rich.

Several years after we had moved to the woods we cashed in our small savings account, stored the kids with their grandparents, and went back to New York on a protracted cultural binge.

One of our teachers at the Art Students' League was George Grosz, who had just made his getaway from Hitler's Germany. When we worked with him he was painting, in watercolor, graceful little nudes against soft and wavy foliage on the Long Island dunes.

He was the most patient of instructors. But he would not be drawn into any discussion of his wartime experiences in the German army or of his cartooning campaigns against capitalists and Nazis.

Someone brought in a copy of his "Ecce Homo" and opened it to a savage caricature. Grosz gave it a quick look. "Oh," he said, "that was so long ago." He closed the book and turned away. He did say once that he and the other early dadaists had started that movement as a joke.

Yasuo Kuniyoshi was also an excellent instructor, but of a different temperament from Grosz. His criticisms would often leave a female student in tears. Sometimes he would fire a burst of curses, then suddenly change to a big, toothy smile, looking exactly like the Japanese general in a World War II cartoon. In fairness to him it should be noted that these were the last years of his life and that he was far from well. We came away with a high opinion of him both as an artist and as a teacher, but his class was hard on tender egos.

Art instruction puts a strain on anybody's equanimity, as I was to learn later. You tramp around the circle of easels, correcting the same old mistakes over and over again. I made a list of these and posted them on the wall: the seven deadly sins that every new student makes. Soon these start to bore a teacher, then annoy him, and finally, if he doesn't watch himself, infuriate him.

The instructor may scream at some innocent beginner who is making one of these errors for the first time, because the poor old guy has been carrying an accumulating burden and this last repetition is the camel-buster.

Kuniyoshi always insisted that New York is the only place for an artist and that landscape painting should be done in the studio rather than on outdoor location. A corollary would be that the best figure painting could be done without a model.

I rejected these ideas at the time, but now I think that there was a good deal of truth in them. New York was where the new ideas were hatching, at that time anyway, and it probably still is. And I have to admit that longer flights of creative imagination can be made under unexciting, neutral conditions than out where we are brought down to earth by the powerful realities of nature.

But the length of these soaring sprees diminishes, and the artist begins to repeat himself if the work is continued too long without recourse to people, places, or things. Then, in my case anyway, either the subject must be brought indoors or I have to go out after it.

Certain limitations must be accepted. It's hard to tear loose from a picture that's coming well, but no watercolor can be completed in the rain.

A canoe is as well suited to watercolor as it is to hunting and fishing. I lay my paddle across the gunwales for a drawing board and have the whole lake to dip my brushes in. No worries about dulling the colors with dirty water. I may drift, putting down impressions of the changing shore. If I want to stay put I drop an anchor tied with two lines, one to the bow and the other to the thwart beside me. That way the boat doesn't swing so wildly as on a single rope, and I can lift the anchor without moving from my place.

Oils may take days to dry, or weeks with some pigments and in some weather. Fay and I would sometimes be paddling with wet paintings laid face-up all over the cargo and carried individually across the portages, a ridiculous sight and an inefficient way to travel. Later we bound them face to face with a few twigs laid between. I might make the last portage packing out a bundle of paintings—hardboard is heavy—with a tump line over my head like a voyageur carrying a bale of fur. The marks that were left by the twigs could be taken out at the studio.

Winter is a good time for painting landscapes in the woods. Winter watercolors can be done from a heated car or truck, but not in the open, because once the water begins to freeze you're through.

Oil is more adaptable. It thickens as the temperature drops but can still be spread on board or canvas. Mittens feel clumsy but don't seem to make the painting any worse. And other threatening circumstances may turn out for the best. I have manipulated a big, wet oil painting through dense hazel brush, trying not to let the surface touch anything, but leaving a trail of brightly colored twigs. That picture looked better after it came out of the thicket than before it went in.

In painting a landscape I find something right about really being a part of the place: shivering or sweating or squinting into the sun or getting bug-bitten. Such small sufferings usually improve the painting. They soak into the wash or work their way into the *impasto*.

Chapter 20

WORD WRASSLER

> If you can meet with triumph and disaster
> And treat those two impostors just the same...
>
> Kipling

That advice was bad for the psyche, we now know. It's better to let our emotions snort, to wail and curse, or to squeal in jubilation. As for that old Victorian, he was a chauvinist, a racist, a sexist and an imperialist.

We understand all that now. But I liked his stuff when I was five years old and I still do.

His two impostors battered my psyche with a wallop in my early days at Exeter. The first shock, though, came as a delightful surprise.

After straining ineffectually for a good part of one night to properly compose an essay due the next morning, I gave up and just wrote freely about an experience I had once had in the woods. Tired though I was, the ordeal suddenly became fun. I quickly finished and went to bed.

Next day I considered throwing it away. But defaulting on a theme when it was due was a worse offense than even the most terrible writing. I waited till others were coming toward the desk with their papers, then laid mine where it would be immediately covered.

That kind of crime, however deeply buried, is soon dug up. I spent an unhappy weekend in repentance. I couldn't afford another failing grade. I was too close to out.

On Monday the stack of corrected papers appeared on Mr. Curwen's desk. He picked one of them up. "I'm going to read this paper to you. You mustn't compare it to Dr. Johnson or Charles Lamb, but for a beginning student, it's good."

He read, and I recognized my opening words, almost in disbelief. I, the dumb shit, social and intellectual misfit, who had been at the bottom of this class as well as all my others, was being suddenly honored.

I tried to keep the calm attitude recommended by Kipling, but I could feel myself expanding, puffing up like a whiskeyjack on a cold morning.

The second thrill came a few minutes later when the papers were handed back. Mine was marked *F* for flunk.

The sad thing dangled, flapping from my hand as I approached the desk.

"I don't understand this grade, Sir."

He patiently pointed out a grammatical error that he had already circled in red. That was all it took to produce a failing grade in any essay.

The incident taught me a principle that I've followed ever since: trust yourself, cut loose, let 'er snort. Don't be ascared of anybody. Work with delight instead of conscientious suffering. It also gave me some badly needed self-confidence. I wasn't worse than all the other guys in *every* department. And one more lesson: when you finish a piece of writing, read it over.

After that at Exeter, and later at Yale, such freely worded themes, essays and reports pleased humanities instructors and brought grades that helped to offset my bad performance in math and the sciences.

On our farm, I chopped vast expanses of brush and shoveled mountains of manure but also typed, painted and drew. My magazine articles on farming, hunting, fishing and camping were all accepted. I sometimes had to send one to several different publications, but they all made it in time.

I also wanted to tell what I knew about the life and culture of the old-time woods Indians. My essays on that subject, and several historical articles, were swiftly and repeatedly rejected by book and magazine publishers. I did contrive to sneak one such piece past the editor. This story of a naval battle on Lake Superior between Sauks and Anishinabeg was published by Blue Book, a fiction magazine. My account wasn't really fiction: just plain old history as told by tribal storytellers. But that material was as exciting as anything a modern writer could invent.

I mailed samples of art work to publishers. There was never any response to these from New York, where almost all the big magazines and most of the little ones were then published, but I did get assignments from Sunday-school papers and other such small stuff in the back country. Some of the pieces they sent me were so badly written that I longed for permission to do a little editing. That was not the job of the illustrator.

An article on goose farming, "They Still Lay Golden Eggs," brought a good check from *Country Gentleman,* then the leading farm publication. It also brought a flood of letters and turned us toward producing goose eggs.

They never had hatched well artificially. Most goose eggs were incubated under setting hens, a small-scale, high-cost operation. We developed a method of hatching them in incubators.

I say we, but I must give Fay most of the credit. Every spring, for several years, she opened every egg that had, under various controlled conditions of moisture and temperature, failed to hatch. She would examine and record the state of development of each dead embryo.

Some of these were well along in decay, and this research was not a pleasant job, but our hatch percentages steadily improved. I wrote a series of bulletins on this and other phases of waterfowl production. These were subjects that had received very little attention in the past. The demand for information was so strong, and the same questions were repeated so often, that we had the answers printed.

This was before women's emancipation had made secretarial work demeaning. Every girl was taught typing in high school. At one time we had sixteen of these student stenographers coming in after hours to answer letters, mail out bulletins, and book orders for eggs, goslings and breeding geese.

We started a quarterly publication, *The Magazine of Ducks and Geese*. The first two issues were finished for us by a printing firm. After that we bought one of the small offset presses that were coming into use for office work. Grace Halverson (Mrs. Hilmer) typed the copy, Ham printed it, and family and helpers joined regularly in frantic efforts to get the copies collated, bound, and mailed out in time to meet the speeding deadlines.

The little press was often sick, stupid, sullen or mischievous, but never slow. If not closely watched it would create errors and then turn out copies like the sorcerer's apprentice. Often Fay and I spent nights with pen or brush correcting the same word in every copy, or modifying, on page after page, some horrendous color.

Almost all magazine articles, then as now, were composed by professional writers proud of their ability to knock out a convincing story on any subject, no matter how little they knew about it. An hour or two in a public library is all they need.

Ours were written by farmers and farm wives who knew ducks and geese but most of whom wouldn't have been able to tell syntax from a participle. I edited the manuscripts freely, even ruthlessly, compacting and revising them into forms that were easy to read and to understand.

The result was a strange publication. Either you loved it or you couldn't believe that it could be so terrible. Several outraged subscribers wrote us in great anger. They got their money back. Most comments ranged from satisfied to ecstatic.

Our subscription list was never big, but we had readers on every continent except Antarctica. One of our best contributors was the manager of a Hungarian collective goose farm. He told, in reasonably understandable English, about production techniques that were unknown in this country, and he was pleased with the information that he got from our magazine.

At his request, we sent payments for his reports in used clothes, any size. These didn't look like much to me but he was delighted to get them. Once, pressed for time, I sent him a money order. He asked me never to do that again: the government charges took almost all of it.

This was in Stalin's time, and the cold war was at its hottest. Our correspondence brought unfavorable reaction on both sides. We got angry letters about publishing communist propaganda. It was worse for Dr. Szepesy. He was formally accused of agricultural espionage. I'm glad to be able to report that he wasn't shot, only demoted.

When, on my father's death, I was drafted into the bank, we sold *D&G*. It had never been very profitable, but it had at least paid small wages and had been a big experience.

During this second session in the bank I felt the need to spend my free time outdoors. I didn't indulge in any writing except for our bank publication, "It's Your Money." Maybe my articles helped people with their financial problems. At least they were different from the usual run of house organ material.

But I did find time for the woods. Fay, Ham, and I took long canoe trips north of the Canadian railroads. Again I was meeting woods Indians. They were still at ease in the forest, more competent than any white man. But the airplane, the outboard motor, the snow machine, and, most of all, the radio were changing them. Old skills, no longer needed, were being forgotten, and practices of the master race were being imitated. The old storytellers were dying off. The manedoog, individualistic and often dangerous spirits that inhabited animals, trees, rocks and waters, were coalescing into Gitchi Manido, a beneficent Indian Jehovah. A beautiful, mysterious, vital American culture was blowing away like an empty bark canoe on Lake Superior.

Most of it was already too far out in the mists for photographs or tape recordings. But not too far for memory. It became the subject of most of my writing and painting.

Some Indians, and some Whites, have been offended by my stories and pictures. In drawings, paintings and words I have described the deep woods Anishinabeg and Cree just the way I saw them: the worn, dirty clothes, the recurrent famines, the many different manedoog.

To me, there was something fine about the combination of extreme poverty and superstition—if it was superstition—with the strength, the determination to survive, and the steady kindness to each other that were characteristic of those people. They had a nobility that is diminished if you pretend that they dressed and acted like pageant Indians.

I have been called a racist, and one of my shows was picketed as such, but I have not altered my pictures or my accounts of the woods Indians as I knew them. They deserved better than that.

Again, an Indian friend tells me that the aadizookaanag are sacred legends, to be told by word of mouth only and not written down for outsiders to read. I respect her opinion, but I don't feel bound by it. I believe that the forest legends are part of the heritage of all mankind. They should not end with the dying breath of the last storyteller.

Chapter 21

DON'T GO NEAR THE WATER

> Into this universe, and why not knowing
> Nor whence, like water willy-nilly flowing
> And out of it, like wind along the waste,
> I know not whither, willy-nilly blowing.
>
> Omar Khayyam

His principal aim was to drown himself. A mature, if melancholy, ambition for a man of 18 months.

His mother had dunked him in the lake soon after they arrived at the bank picnic, then had tried to interest him in other pursuits. These were no go. As soon as he was deposited in some safe place he started hitching and crawling toward the beach and right into the water until somebody dragged him back. Then patiently, relentlessly, he repeated the attempt.

Maybe I'm giving my great grandson credit for too advanced a philosophy. Maybe, if they'd let him alone, he would have been satisfied just to soak in the shallows. Or else to have gone swimming off across the lake.

Friends of ours have lost children in the water. It happens often enough to keep parents cautious.

The lakes, streams and swamps that lace this northern country are an attractive menace. A creek that would hardly ooze through your shoes in August turns into a torrent in April. Kids love to puddle in wet places at all seasons.

The best protection seems to be to get them swimming early. They take to it like other little animals. My own instruction was so far back that I can't remember it. I have a clear memory picture of my brother Newton dog-paddling happily out of my father's arms at some ridiculous baby age.

Fay was prompt in teaching our children and grandchildren to swim. They quickly got the two basic understandings: that you don't breathe when you're submerged and that water lifts you, if you will let it.

Canoe education, too, began early. Ham was nine months old when Fay tucked him into a padded nest in the bow beside the dock at Beaudette, a frontier town then, on the Lake of the Woods. I was stowing the packs and other gear in place.

We were unconscious of any wrongdoing until the comments of bystanders became pointedly hostile.

"Do they really intend to take that baby out on the lake in a canoe?"

"What's the matter with you men? Are you just going to stand around and let them do it?"

"There must be some law against this kind of thing!" Someone hurried loudly off to summon the authorities.

We didn't argue, but speeded the launching. It was a relief to have water open between us and that bon voyage committee.

As we neared the breakwater two bark canoes passed us, headed for town. They were loaded down close to the water level with cargo that included plenty of puppies and babies. Nobody would be scolding them.

I might have shouted back over the waves some comment about racial discrimination. Except that I had never heard that expression and the folks on the wharf wouldn't have known what I was talking about.

On a May morning three years later I was giving Ham a paddling-alone lesson in front of my parents' cottage. I showed him that sitting in the bow seat while facing what is ordinarily the stern puts a person's weight closer to the center of the canoe, balancing, to some extent, the lack of a partner paddler.

In the afternoon he induced his grandfather to take him out again. The wind had come up, so they kept to the lee shore. When they came back my father pulled the gray canoe well up on the beach.

At supper time, Ham was missing. Fay and I looked at each other, then ran for the lake. The only sign of the canoe was a long groove in the sand.

The family rowboat, dried and leaky from winter storage, was soaking on the lake bottom, loaded with stones.

Fay went sprinting down the shore to get help. Father and I waded out to the sunken boat, lifted the rocks from it, dragged it up on the beach, dumped the water out of it, and pushed it back into the lake. All this effort had a surreal, dreamlike feeling. One of those dreams where you are trying hard and moving slowly.

We were finally afloat, I at the oars, Father paddling and steering from the stern. Facing him, I watched his eyes turning to the right and the left, searching the lake, finding nothing. Then he squinted, focused on one spot. I stopped rowing for a moment, turned my head to that direction.

The waves were breaking white against some floating thing way off to starboard. He ruddered our boat around toward it, then paddled hard as I heaved on the oars.

I paused and looked again. Now I could see it. A capsized gray hull, tossing, bottom up.

No hope now. But keep on, straining, despairing strokes. It must be close. I turned again.

I saw weathered planking, not silver-gray canvas. Some other boat had been torn away by the wind. Our boy may be alive yet!

Meanwhile, Fay was running along the shore, climbing over fences, splashing through streams, pounding and shouting at locked doors.

There was no telephone. Many people hadn't arrived yet for the summer season. Some had no boats. One man had painted his and, after thinking it over, decided that he might damage the job by putting it into the water. Others wouldn't risk going out in such weather.

Fay knew that she had no time to beg or argue. When she was refused at one house she turned away in silence and ran on to the next. Once she fainted and came back to consciousness lying on the sand. Not a single boat but ours put out that evening.

We crossed the main body of the lake without seeing anything more but stormy water and distant shore. The wind led us on down a long bay. As we neared the end of it Father called out that there was something in the reeds ahead. Then that it was the gray canoe. Then that Ham was in it.

He was sitting in the bow seat, facing the stern as instructed, still trying to paddle, but unable, in that wind, to turn the canoe, or control it in any way. He was crying a little. It had been a fast ride over a long distance.

We shouted to him to sit still and keep low. More rowing. Then at last we were alongside and lifting him into the rowboat.

I got into the canoe and we headed for home. That heavy pull into the waves was a joyful trip for us, but Fay was still running along the shore searching for help. She saw us coming across the water and met us at the beach. She spent the next two days in bed.

Kids get older and you think, they'll be all right now, but they find ways to scare you just the same.

Beryl found one on a pleasant summer day. One of those balmy days when a wind from down south in Wisconsin came across 'Tschgumi, rolling big waves of surface water in to warm the frigid bays of the north shore.

We were having a family picnic in the shelter of a tall dike. A dike, on this coast, is a wall not made by men but formed by a river of magma, melted rock, that once flowed through a fissure between two sections of earlier and softer stone. These restraining banks were worn away during the millennia, leaving a vertical wall of granite that extends out into the lake.

The waves and currents, in their choosy fashion, had left one side of this barrier clear, forming a bay that ran back some two hundred feet to the shore boulders. The lake had filled in the other side of the dike with small stones to make a curving shore.

On this pebble beach we built a fire and cooked meat. The rock wall stood seven feet above us, was about ten feet wide, and ran down to some unknown depth on the bay side.

It provided a good shelter from the wind. After lunch Fay and I lay back beside it to enjoy the sun. The children, rushing the waiting period a little, waded out into the lake. Ham was fifteen and Beryl thirteen. They were both good swimmers. We didn't think they needed watching.

We were just snoozing off in our warm corner when, above the sound of the surf, there came a frightened wail from the other side of the dike. I ran along its side, found a cleft, and scrambled up. When I reached the top I was horrified to see Beryl in the waves beyond, close to where they were breaking against vertical rocks. She had swum around the lake end of the dike.

I hesitated. We hadn't been swimming here before. I didn't know how deep the water was or what kind of bottom lay below it.

But the very size of the rollers passing beneath me was reassuring. Peering down into their troughs I could see no dark shapes, warnings of submerged rocks. If I timed my plunge to catch the crest of a big one, it should give enough depth, no matter what might be further down. As the next white ridge swelled up beneath me I went into it, driving hard with my legs, aiming far out, and arching my back to make the shallowest dip possible.

I touched no stone and came to the surface traveling fast and well on my way toward the blond head in the waves. I reached her with a few strokes. I had never been in this kind of surf before and had no idea what I was going to do to get us out of it.

In the next few minutes I discovered some interesting facts about hydraulics. Beryl was still in the same place, not much closer to the rocks than she had been when I stood on the dike. I could feel very little shoreward pressure.

Any kind of boat would have been hurled against the rocks and quickly converted into kindling. We swimmers offered almost no surface to the wind. The water was deep, and we were in a fairly vertical position, so that our legs and most of our bodies were below

the rolling surface. Down there the action was working up and down rather than sweeping in from the lake. Although we were frighteningly close to the surf and stone, we were not being swept toward them. Beryl was scared, but otherwise in good shape. She wasn't bruised, and she hadn't taken in any water.

We never talked about the incident until a few days ago. I was preparing to write this story and asked her if she remembered it. She said that she'd never forget it, but that she had felt safe as soon as she saw me in the water. Father would take care of her.

Father had not been so confident. He had, in fact, been just as scared as she was. But it had soon become clear that neither of us was in any danger. No rescue was needed. We just swam together, rising and falling in the waves, around the dike and back to the beach.

When we got to our feet in the shallow water we did get a little rough treatment. The playful breakers tumbled us both on the pebbles. That's no more than you expect in surf swimming.

Chapter 22

MEETINGS WITH MUKWA

> I follow bears
> over the bush-grown mother rock
> where bushes fruit Juneberries
> big as grapes and sweet.
> Here and there a bush is mangled,
> bear-crushed, broken.
> —Pull the bush down
> Strip
> with clawed hands. Stuff leaves, fruit
> onto a blue tongue.
>
> Joanne Hart

Susan Red Sky is firm. "We can't take the dog, Margaret."

"Oh, don't worry about Jacko. See how quietly he sits there. All those buckets around him, and all those kids, and he doesn't bother any of them."

The Anishinabe women don't answer. Margaret, Susan's guest from outside the reservation, looks around, finds no support in their faces.

"I've got to have Jacko. Because I'm deathly afraid of bears. We might meet one in the blueberry bush."

"That's just it," says Susan. "We probably will. Bears like berries too, but they don't get along with dogs. If Mukwa comes, I'll talk to him. He won't mind moving off a ways. There will be berries enough for all of us. Sister-in-law, just call Jacko out of the car."

Margaret stands, defiantly silent. Another woman speaks.

"The old people hunted the hairy uncle for meat and the sweet white grease, but they never bothered him when they didn't need to. That can bring misfortune on a family. If the dog goes, I'm staying here."

"You can leave Jacko in my house," someone offers.

Reluctantly, Margaret agrees.

A guarded alliance between bears and men, and a mystic understanding between bears and women, have always been evident to the people of the northern forests, not just in America, but also in ancient Britain, in Scandinavia, Siberia, and the upper islands of Japan.

A bear has big teeth, long curved claws and many times greater strength than the most powerful man. He can easily destroy a person, and yet he seldom attacks us. He never runs in herds or packs, but hunts and gathers as we do. He lives, like us, on vegetation, seeds, roots, and meat. He stands and walks like us. His body, when skinned, looks like one of ours. His paws resemble our hands and feet, and he uses them as we do. He understands what we say.

Long ago, a female bear graciously permitted a man to mate with her. That is the reason for the similarities of the two species. But in certain ways, bears are more godlike.

The great star-bear moves through the northern sky, turning the eternal wheel, the spokes and rim of night and day, to take the sun away every evening and bring it safely back at morning.

When winter comes, bears go into the earth, seem to die. But they are guarding the cave, the womb of the world, the passageway of new life. At the proper time, they and their newborn young come out of that sacred tunnel.

A man should avoid these mysteries before any serious effort. To kill a bear or to have sexual intercourse with a woman has brought disaster to war parties.

Bears may be hunted, but only in the formal way, with prayers and explanations before, and with thanks after. If we do this, and if we treat the bones honorably, the bear comes back to life.

Even a white man, or a white man's Indian, dulled and corrupted by civilization, can see that this animal is special.

ଔଞ୍ଚ

It takes all kinds of bears to make a world. Most of them are intent on minding their own business and keeping out of trouble. This majority are not interested in messing around with people.

Sometimes, crossing a portage on a hot, still day, you get a sniff of the musky odor of a bear. Then you know that Mukwa has politely and silently stepped into the woods, turning over the trail to you. If you don't like his smell you can be certain that he is even less enthusiastic about yours.

We had finished the chores and were sitting in front of the tent on a bluff that dropped down to a broad bay. A full moon floated up into the sky out of 'Tschgumi.

Fay leaned forward. "What's that?"

A ripple had come slicing into the bright moon-path leaving a widening strip of darkness. At its point we could make out the face and ears of a bear, bobbing up and down a little with the swimming effort, moving fast. He was crossing from the headland on one side of our camp to that on the other side.

"That's a long traverse," I said. "He must have urgent business over there to take that swim in such cold water."

"No matter how pressing the business, if I'd been in his place, I'd have taken the inland detour."

"There's a little breeze coming over the lake from the South that would carry our scent way back into the hills. If he'd gone that way he'd have had to put up with that unpleasant and worrisome human odor."

The ripple left the shaft of light and became bright in the darkness. It never slowed or turned until it reached the distant shore.

Visitors from Europe fear Indian attack. Those from American cities are more worried about bears. They come armed with heavy revolvers, portage to the accompaniment of banging pans and request light and company when they go to the latrine at night.

Such precautions seem excessive to us natives, but the opposite—the teddy-bear reaction—is worse. Bears are not to be hand-fed like chipmunks or whiskey-jacks.

We once chased a bear across a bay of a northern lake. Ham was paddling. Fay and I were making quick sketches, picking up our paddles to help him when we got behind.

The bear paid no attention to us until he had climbed out on the rocks. Then he turned and faced us. The hair was plastered down tight over the lean, wild-animal body, showing powerful muscles. He was not growling. He was all done being chased, though. We were separated from him by a strip of water, but we were close. There is nothing cute or cuddly about a wet bear at that distance.

Back in college days I invited my roommate to come up for a canoe trip. It took some urging, on account of the bears. But Bill finally decided to take the risk. He arrived on the same day that a bear chose to invade our city's best hotel.

Wild animals are not uncommon in Duluth. Bears tip over garbage cans in the suburbs. A deer may follow a stream-side park down from the hills and then move off confusedly into traffic. A good many muskrats and an occasional lynx are trapped in the swampy wasteland along the edges of St. Louis Bay. I can remember dashing to the school window, along with everybody else in the disrupted class, to watch a moose run down the sidewalk.

But a bear in the Hotel Duluth lobby was a first. He followed the smell of breakfast bacon into the coffee shop and was shot there by the police. The story was all over the front page of the newspaper.

The only way I could keep my guest from taking the next train south was to lie a little bit. Well, not lie, really, but equivocate.

I told him that there would be plenty of islands and promised that we would camp each night on one of them. He didn't ask about bears as swimmers. I thought that we were unlikely to get close to any of them on this particular trip.

How wrong I was!

As we turned off the highway toward our starting point the first bear rose out of the brush beside the logging road to greet us. Another stood on the beach and watched us paddle past. Several days later we saw one swimming across a lake.

Bill was a photographer. This bear seemed harmless, intent only on keeping out of our way and getting to land as fast as he could. I heard the camera clicking as I cut in ahead of him. He swung around and headed back for the opposite shore.

Bill's hunting instinct was now aroused. He grabbed up his paddle.

"Head him off and I'll shoot him some more!"

With both paddles flashing we swept past the fugitive and brought the canoe to a shuddering halt in his path.

The expression on the bear's face changed from anxiety to determination. Enough of this chasing back and forth!

This time he kept right on swimming. His claws hooked into the cedar of the gunwale. The streaming black body swung up the side like a Malay pirate boarding a junk. The canoe jerked down into a crazy tilt, swallowing water.

Bill and I threw our weight far over on the other side. The bear kept right on coming. Bill swung the paddle up and slugged at his head. The gunwale dipped again.

I set my paddle against the bear's shoulder, braced myself, and pushed. We teetered crazily. A lot of water was sloshing around our feet.

For a few minutes we hung there, the three of us silently clawing, shoving and battering. I thought that we would soon all be together, either in the canoe or in the lake.

Suddenly the boarding party let go. We almost capsized in the opposite direction then lurched back into soggy, rocking equilibrium.

The bear was already well on his way to shore. He would not bother us any more. Nobody would get in his path this time. Mukwa is a reasonable animal. We had reached an understanding.

As the sun came down toward the trees that afternoon, Bill said, "Never mind about the island."

A week later we crossed the divide at the farthest-out point in our circle of waterways, portaged into a river that flowed south, and followed it to a deep lake surrounded by enormous boulders.

We pitched our tent on the top of one of these. I crawled in first, felt around in the deep moss to find the more level side, and rolled up in my blanket. The other half of the enclosed space was considerably tilted with a deep break in the rock just inside the door. Bill did the best he could to level off his bed by jamming the food pack into this little gully to hold up his feet.

That was why he waked first. The pack woke him. It was trying not to. Quietly, gently, inch by inch, it was moving out from under.

His first thought was that I was up early and getting breakfast. But when he looked over at my side of the tent, there I was sleeping peacefully.

For one horrified moment he closed his eyes again. Then he opened them and looked down.

I felt his grip squeezing my shoulder hard. He breathed into my ear, "John. Wake up. There's a bear."

I was sleepily annoyed.

"Well don't bother me now about nature observation. Just go ahead and observe him. Get your camera and go out and shoot him when it's light enough.

The reply came in a whisper. "I don't have to go out. He's here

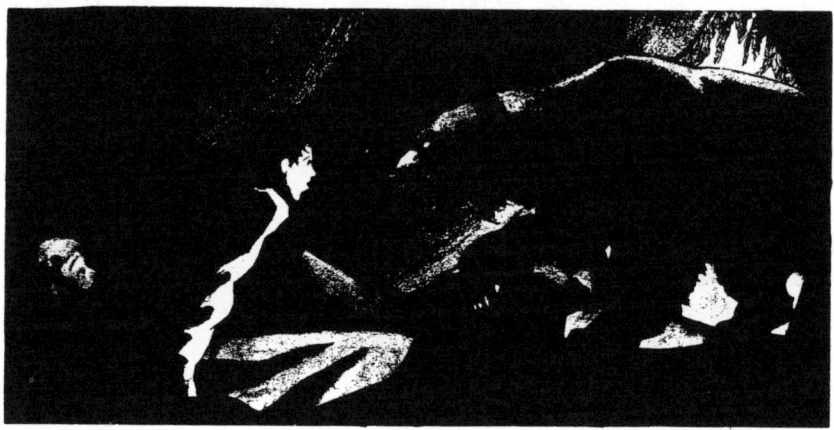

in the tent."

I jackknifed into a sitting position. A dark shape was silhouetted against the stars between trailing shreds of mosquito netting.

The bear seemed to realize that there was no more need for caution. He pulled the food pack clear, then rose to his hind feet. He stood there, his head lifting the tent canvas. He was squeezing the pack against his belly, trying to decide whether that would be enough. Should he take one of us along for good measure?

My breath came back to me. Enough for a hysterical yelp. It was not a brave or threatening sound. But the bear must have been nervous, too. He dropped the pack, scooted across the moss, and disappeared over the edge of the boulder.

A bundle of dry bark and pine kindling had been stored for the night against possible showers. Bill snatched this package and scrambled out of the tent. A flame glowed, then lighted up the rocks around us, and shone back from the birch trunks that leaned in over our stone hill.

We felt braver, but not enough to wait for breakfast. Bill poured gear and blankets into the packs. I hurried to get the tent down, while keeping watch on the thicket below.

There was a movement there in the spruce branches. I stood staring down, my arms full of limp canvas.

The bear rose out of the bush, looked at me, dropped to all fours, and came firmly up the side of the rock. I pushed a curl of birch bark into the fire, then stepped down to meet him, waving the flaring thing before me.

He stopped and made a nasty face at me, rolling back his upper lip and clicking his teeth. He slapped the ground hard with his front foot. His hand, the Anishinabeg would say.

In this confrontation I felt a certain familiar bluffage. As a child, on my way home from school, I had to pass a house owned by a big dog. Every day he would come roaring out at me. If I ran he would give me a painful nip. If I bent over and picked up a stone he would stop, and would continue to denounce me from a safe distance.

The bear was bigger than the dog but not so mean. He had no grudge against us. He just wanted the groceries.

We were too far out now to part with these easily. Fish and berries are fine, but you need some fat too to fuel all that paddling and portaging. I would try to face the bear down. He couldn't have the bacon slab unless he absolutely insisted.

He seemed to have figured out the situation about the same as I had. He started up the rock, looking determined, but not in a real rush.

Bill stood beside me holding the light axe that was our nearest thing to a weapon. I knew that, scared as he was, he would whack it into the bear if he had to.

The black uncle was close now. With the fry pan I scooped up some live coals and burning twigs and tossed them in his direction, but not close enough to singe him. He stopped but gave a blood-chilling growl. I decided not to do any more of that.

By this time the lake was brightening under the pre-dawn sky. Maybe the bear was bothered by the growing daylight. He backed down to ground level, then prowled around the rock. Sometimes he disappeared into the trees. Sometimes he started up at us. Then we faced him with shouts and bold gestures.

We had finished packing now, ready to escape if we could, but we hesitated to give up the high ground.

At last, when the bear was on the side farthest from the lake, we looked at each other, nodded, grabbed up the bundles. Still barefoot and in our long underwear sleeping costumes, we ran and slid down the slope, whipped the canoe into the water, and tossed in the packs. Bill jumped into the bow. I gave a flying shove from the stern. The bear came galloping around the boulder. We shot, rocking and veering, out into the morning stillness of the lake. He stood watching from the shore, looking sad as a deserted lover.

On the far side of the next portage we stopped long enough to get dressed and eat a cold breakfast. The canoe lay packed in the water, ready for a quick departure. We ate standing beside it and watching the woods. The bear hadn't followed.

ఇళ

The clean, ivory-colored skull of a bear is now a prop in my studio. I have wired the jaw in place to keep it from dropping out, and have cemented loose teeth back into their sockets.

To me it is beautiful form in the pursuit of function. The masterly design is evident—the bone thickened at each stressful point where reinforcement is needed to give maximum strength with minimum weight. But when I set it on a draped pedestal for a still-life class there were always gasps of distress from a few of the students.

The original owner, or tenant, of this bone hung around our farm for two months. She moved quietly and seldom allowed herself to be seen, but she let us know that she was there.

We had cut a road back through the woods and had fenced in partly cleared fields on both sides of it. At each gate were steel barrels filled with a mixture of ground grain, dried milk, and meat scrap. The bear would upset these and eat what she wanted, leaving quite a lot spread over the ground. Every time she climbed a fence—and that was whenever she took the notion to get to the other side—her weight tore the woven wire down off the posts, leaving such wreckage that she might as well have just walked through it.

I was afraid that she would get tired of the mash and start on our livestock. Some bears do, although it's unusual. I used to walk back evenings to make sure that everything was all right. I never saw her on one of those strolls, but sometimes I smelled her or heard the wire fence creak under her weight. She never bothered our birds or animals.

When the apples ripened she took to coming into the yard around the house at night. We couldn't see her black bulk in the darkness. Sometimes she stood still until we were quite close to her, and then went crashing off through the brush.

Fay, Beryl, and Ham got used to her presence, but some of the neighbors' kids wouldn't even walk past our place. When Beryl had a birthday party, Fay had to meet the guests and see them safely off the premises afterwards, convoying them through the bear zone.

Our income was small. Torn fences and spilled feed were getting expensive. I took to carrying a rifle when I walked out back. One afternoon I caught the bear in the open and shot her.

She was excellent eating. Like good beef, but with more marbling. In the next few weeks I put on weight that took me years to shed. Speaking from this experience, I'd say that a really serious danger that people have to fear from confrontations with bears is getting fat.

In recent years Fay has had a good many meetings with Mukwa. The other day she walked into the bedroom and found one of them poking his head in through an open window. "Go home!" she ordered. He shuffled off obediently into the woods.

An old-time Anishinabe might have spoken more politely to get the same result. But a white woman may be excused for being a little abrupt with a bear in her bedroom. Goldilocks in reverse.

Chapter 23

IN THE CRADLE OF THE DEEP

> Cushion me soft.
> Rock me in the billowy drowse.
> > Whitman

The almost-full carton of milk had been set into a crevice in the shore rocks where the water, washing in and out, would keep it cold. Now, when everybody was ready to eat, it had slipped its moorings.
 There it is!
 Right side up and bobbing out there in the lake. The offshore breeze was moving it farther. I volunteered to do a dog's job and retrieve it.
 About three strokes, outward bound, changed that intention. I lost all interest in errant milk. All I wanted was to get out of that water.
 And then to bend over the fire, almost caressing it. Sail on, yellow carton.
 Even in hot summer, along his rocky north shore, 'Tschgumi holds his grip on winter. His ice melts, but his water doesn't warm.

Little kids can take it for a while, especially fat little kids. When you reach high school age there's no use pretending that you can swim in it.

If the air is still and the sun is really roasting you, you may plunge in for relief. Instant relief, and you plunge right out, chilled blue.

Swimming becomes possible when a strong wind piles up surface water against a shore. This condition happens quite often on the long curve of the Point. But there is a catch to it. It takes a northeast wind, and that usually means cold and windy weather.

This kind of day is not favored by either swimmers or sunbathers. You look north and then south over that expanse of sand and see nobody.

You look far but not long. It's too chilly. And you certainly won't linger in the shallows after the first breaker soaks you. You hustle for deep water, hopping over the smaller waves and leaning far forward against the big ones to keep them from bowling you over backwards.

Once ducked and afloat, you find the water surprisingly comfortable. All that sun-warmed upper layer from way out in the lake has been shoved in here by the wind. But you must watch each incoming hill, so that an unexpected upswing won't catch you inhaling. Soon you are timing strokes and breathing to conform to the rise and fall of the surface without even thinking about it.

Waves of a northeaster often get higher than twenty feet from trough to crest. As they approach the shore they trip over the bottom and tip forward, breaking into surf. You mustn't struggle to stay on top of them. Just let each big surge pass over you.

No matter how fiercely wind and water may be raging overhead, it's always peaceful down here. You lie, suspended, cushioned in the billowy drowse, waiting for the next trough to bring you to the surface. Or, rather, to bring the surface down to you. When that happens there is time to take several unhurried breaths and then to fill your lungs before you are again submerged.

You can paddle along for hours and go as far out in the lake as you please, so long as you submit to the rhythm of the waves instead of fighting against it. The routine is like some fairy story where the hero is safe from the most fearsome dangers so long as he carries out the sorcerer's instructions.

If you're used to swimming in ocean surf, you have no trouble here. Most midwesterners are not accustomed to steep waves. And very few know that they have these cold-air, warm-water, windswept opportunities.

After a number of failures we worked out a way to launch a canoe from the beach into a northeaster. We waded in, Fay on one side in front, I on the other in back, holding the boat between us. We moved as quickly as possible through this carrying zone. But we stopped and braced ourselves as each breaker struck, lifting the canoe so that it would not be filled and so that its weight would press our feet to the sand and keep us from being tipped over. At the right time, just after one of these big waves had passed, we set the boat down and hopped in fast to meet the next wave paddling.

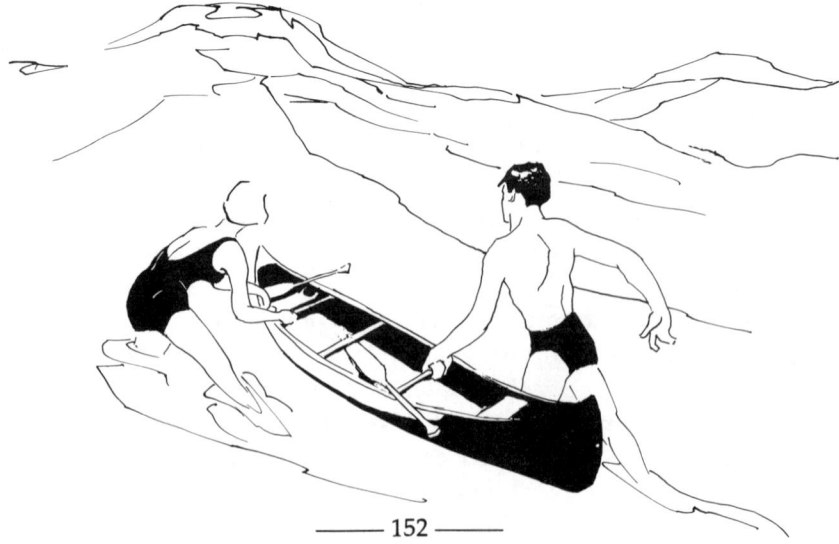

Fay knelt behind the front seat, leaving the bow light enough to clear the breaking crests without shipping much water. We had to hold a course close to the wind, eighthing into it, if I may use such a word, instead of the usual quartering. A quarter angle away from a head-on approach gave the wind too much grip on our high bow. Even at an eighth we both had to dig in hard on the lee side.

When and if we made it through the whitecaps to the deep water, the going got easier. Out here the waves were even bigger, but stable, not yet falling forward, less eager to break into the boat.

We might paddle some distance over them, then turn and run down the wind to shore. As we rode the forward slope of one of these giants we moved at thrilling speed. For a time the canoe would act as a surf board. It drew more water than a board, so eventually the wave got away from under it. But there was always the next one coming up from behind to take over.

Often we came in clinging to the swamped hull. Any time on the outgoing trip that we got careless or winded so that we faltered a little, we lost our tight angle into the waves. Instantly the bow was swept down wind and the next breaker struck us broadside, filling the boat or capsizing it.

As it went over I always felt an instinctive urge to jump clear. But if we left the canoe before it was well filled with water the wind might catch it and flip it through the air for some unpredictable distance, away from us maybe, or worse, at us. Fay got a spectacular bruise that way, a dark diagonal streak across her thigh. After that we made it a rule to stay put until we were solidly flooded.

Once overboard, all we had to do was hang on. Even when we upset far out in the lake, the wind and the waves soon set us, boat and all, back on the beach. Then we had to snatch it out of the water in a hurry. Each wave was scraping the bottom, scooping up sand. Just one of them might dump such a load into the canoe that it would look as though it had been part of the shoreline for years.

We enjoyed this sport for several summers and introduced other people to it. One of these was Norman, our son-in-law. Beryl had hooked this catch out of Lake Superior when he incautiously went ashore for a blind date while his ship was being loaded with ore. He became as keen as we were about canoeing in the surf.

Then, within a few days, we had two near-drownings.

Fay was sketching on the beach. Norm and I were in the canoe. For the first time in my life I was wearing a life jacket, one of the old-fashioned kind with oblong pieces of cork sewn into the canvas. You wrap it around your torso and tie it there with heavy canvas wicks.

We had found this one washed up in the sand. It was worn and ragged, but not rotten. I put it on for no reason that I can think of except that it made me feel virtuously conventional.

We made our way out to the edge of the breakers, then did something wrong and capsized. Rather than staying with the ship I struck out to try my new equipment.

The first big wave, instead of sweeping smoothly over me, grabbed me by the jacket, hoisted me over its shoulder, and then rolled me along on its roaring, churning crest.

From that point on I have only a vague mind-picture, a soused memory of being wrapped and whirled in white water, shaken, revolved, battered. And flooded.

Trying to breathe, I got not air but water.

I scrabbled to get the jacket off. It held on strong and tight: no give, not the least loosening.

Where were the bindings? I searched with frantic fingers. At last they found a knot. It was solid, unyielding, without mercy.

Memory deserts me here. I cannot tell you how I did it. Recognition of close-in death can multiply a man's powers. Somehow I tore free from the embrace of that murderous lifesaver.

I dropped below the stormy surface. But dropped, this time, like a can full of water. Down and down.

And now there was no sanctuary in the depths. I had to get air.

Swimming hard I stopped the downward sag, held level for a while, struggled slowly up. A trough came swooping down. My head broke the foam-streaked curve of its surface. A little air worked down into my waterlogged breathing machinery. The next hill buried me deep, moved slowly above me, and rolled on.

Gasping and choking during the above-water intervals I clung to the desperate edge of consciousness. I tried to call for help. No breath for that. Not even a squeak. Nothing in sight but the towering waves.

Fay, on the beach all this time, and Norm, hanging to the canoe, had no idea that I was in trouble.

People who tell you that drowning is an easy death are not speaking from experience. Without air I was without strength. My efforts slowed. I was hardly able to keep from sinking.

I had lost touch with the rhythm of the waves. Dragging in a little air I was suddenly refilled with water. The friendly drowse had turned into a deadly enemy.

I don't know how I stayed alive and afloat. I suppose that I regained my timing so that I gasped at the right moments. But I can't remember it. I can't remember anything except a dim, desperate struggle.

The waves were carrying me in. Barely conscious, I felt my hand touch bottom. Then the undertow, the backwash from the beach, swept me out and under.

My arms and legs must have gone on working because after a while I was sprawled, face down, on hard, wet sand. The lake was still surging up and trying to grab me but not getting hold enough to drag me back.

I lay there gasping, crawled a little farther, and lay still again, now beyond the reach of the waves. Finally I was really breathing. My people came looking for me. It must have all happened in a much shorter time than it seemed.

A few days after this incident a friend of mine had another bad water trip. He had come down to the Point with some of our family to canoe in the surf. They capsized, and he filled up with water just the way I had or worse. This time, Norm saw that he was in trouble. He and a nephew of mine got him to shore and worked on him till he was breathing again.

We all seemed to lose interest in the game after that.

Chapter 24

SPIRITS BENEATH THE ICE

> But beneath, the evil spirits
> Lay in ambush waiting for him
> Broke the treacherous ice beneath him
> Dragged him downward to the bottom
> Of the Lake of Gitche Gumee.
>
> Longfellow

We had been halted by a tangled mass of bleached timber, pale in the gathering darkness. The sawlogs stood as though frozen in an act of violence—long dead, but still holding their rebellious postures.

The river men would have been watching this sharp bend. The jam must have reared up so fast and locked so solidly into the rock that they couldn't budge it with pikepoles or dynamite. It would stay there for as many years as time, decay, and spring floodwaters might take to sweep it away.

We could go no farther that night. I cleared a space between two pines and tied the tent to their trunks. Fay brought in wood and cooked supper.

    We had just finished eating when we heard the soft sigh of a canoe beached in the sand beneath us. An old woodsman had seen our fire. He came climbing up the bank for a visit. It wasn't hard to get him talking about the early times.
    Late one winter, while tending a trap line along this same stream, he had felt the ice give way beneath him.

The current was strong with the urgency of coming spring. By the time he had kicked off his snowshoes, torn the traps from his waist, and pulled out of his parka, he had been carried far down the river.

He struggled up against the ice, battering at it with his hands, but was unable to break through. Desperate, he pushed his face against it. Right there he found a little space between ice and water, a bite of air.

He made his way upstream, swimming, clawing at the snow-darkened ceiling. At last he saw dim light ahead. As he struggled toward it, it became a shaft of sunlight coming down through the hole where he had broken through.

This was at a point where the river narrowed. The faster current here had thinned the ice. The edges gave way under his weight as he tried to lift himself. He broke his way through to where the water was slower and the ice thicker. There he climbed out. He was dangerously chilled, but he got to a spruce thicket, broke off some dry twigs, opened a wax-sealed packet of matches, and started a fire. The men of those days were not easy to kill.

A picture comes to mind of another frozen river. A group of kids are playing hockey. One of them breaks through. He is unable to climb out on the yielding ice.

An older boy knows what to do. Obeying his orders we spread-eagle ourselves on the ice, each extending a hockey stick to the next. The chain of bodies linked by grasped sticks applies minimum downward pressure at any one point.

The farthest-out pushes his stick to the one in the river. He grabs it. As he clambers out, the ice around the hole cracks and the water comes flooding up out of it. Two more boys are soaked now, but the chain holds. Soon the ice is clear and the wet ones are being rushed to the nearest house.

Forest travel is interrupted in late autumn when the waterways freeze, break open, and freeze again. This may continue for weeks. When everything is solid, traffic resumes, first on foot and by dog sled, later by snow machine or tractor train. If you are unfamiliar with the ways of ice, you must be careful.

The bridge toll between Duluth and Superior was fifteen cents for one man and one vehicle plus five cents for each passenger. These unconscionable rates inspired people to take chances during the newly frozen period. When real winter set in they might as well have closed the bridge.

Very cautious persons didn't take the ice route until New Year's day. By that time, used Christmas trees had been set up in the snow to mark the safe route. Safe, that was, until the channel current, gnawing from below, came too close to the thawing caused by the spring sun above.

People were so reluctant to start paying tribute again that they wouldn't use the bridge until some truck or automobile had taken the plunge.

Surprisingly often the occupants would survive. Sometimes a couple of wheels would break through and there would be time to jump out and get away to firm ice. If somebody went down with the ship he would probably pop up again and be fished out by the next in line. Most of the cars in those days had canvas tops and were open on the sides, easier to get out of than the closed-in kind we drive now. Also, the current in the bay was less concentrated than that in the canal, not so hungry to snatch away potential victims.

Sailors say that when an ore carrier breaks up in a December storm you may as well ride the ship down because there is no chance to live in that cold water. I am told that when you ride a modern automobile down, the correct procedure is to sit tight until the water level inside rises to the top of a door. By then the pressure, so they say, is equalized so that you can open the door and leave.

Well, I don't know about that. You wouldn't be sitting, because a car upends in water, the front end pulled down by the weight of the motor. A car with all the windows closed will usually float for a while, back end up. I've never had the experience myself, but I guess I'd be trying to get out while it was still bobbing.

In planning for such an event, it's well to keep in mind that when really bad things happen to us their details are likely to be different from what we expected. We have to practice for emergencies as well as theorize. But I don't see how we can practice for this one. Maybe it's better just to keep off doubtful ice.

Nobody drives across the frozen bay any more. I can't reproach today's men with timidity on that account, because now we have a toll-free bridge.

The woods Indians, of course, were the real experts in the mysteries of ice, as they were in every other phase of wilderness existence. They couldn't afford the luxury of just staying off it: hunting and gathering had to go on. Their language had a word for each of the many types of ice that develop in changing weather. They sensed danger as wild animals do and, like them, ran risks only when these were necessary for survival.

The loggers of early times were not so expert as the Indians, but knew more about ice than anybody does today. As winter dragged on and the need for a trip to town became imperative, they sometimes took what looked like long chances. They usually got away with them.

In crossing rotten ice one man would walk ahead, picking his way carefully, tapping with his axe at bad-looking spots. Another would follow at a safe distance, carrying a long pole. If the front man broke through, the tip of the pole would be there for him when he came up. He would hang to it with one hand, and to his axe with the other, while he climbed and was dragged through breaking ice and out of the water.

Most breakthroughs happen soon after the freezeup or when the weather starts to warm in the spring. Midwinter cold, though, doesn't guarantee safety.

Chink and I were driving a pickup truck with speed and confidence over hard-frozen January ice, up the slim northern arm of Crane lake that stretches out to Canada. Suddenly I saw a dark spot in the white drifts ahead. I braked. The truck slued on the slippery surface. I let up on the brake to pull her out of the skid, braked again, easier this time, and came to a stop uncomfortably close to the water. A strong current was gurgling through the narrows between Crane and Sandpoint Lakes, keeping this spot open regardless of calendar and thermometer.

We drove up a side bay, drained the crankcase oil into a can and set off on snowshoes for a cold but happy week of hunting, hiking, and camping.

When we came back we heated the oil over a fire and poured the hot stuff back into the motor. This was our procedure on a winter trip. It gave us a quick and easy start no matter how long the truck had been standing, or how low the temperature had fallen.

We had driven about half a mile south when we felt the ice give under us, let us distinctly downwards. What you might correctly call a sinking feeling. The whole surface of the long bay seemed to have lowered. Water had come up over the ice and was level with our floorboards.

We hadn't sunk. Not all the way. The only thing we could think

of to do was to keep on going.

Chink, who still hadn't learned to swim, crawled back into the box, ready for a quick jump if that should seem advisable. I propped the door open and drove as fast as the truck would go. It had a bone in its teeth, as the sailors say: a spill of white rolling out from the prow. A fine wavy wake spread out behind.

The ice held, smooth and firm under the water. For all I know, we might have been able to drive a ten-ton truck over it. But I was glad to reach the landing, take my shivering partner into the cab, and convert the ice-covered machine back from a motor boat to a vehicle.

It's not unusual for ice to sink under the weight of a heavy fall of snow, but that's usually thin ice in early winter. I'd never seen any other sinkage so deep or so extensive as this.

Some years later when I had reached a more discreet age, Fay presented me with a new ice problem. She had become interested in figure skating, seeing in it the possibility of an extension of the dance into a different art form.

She didn't waste any time about getting at this project when the lakes had frozen. She quickly developed a good understanding of ice. I really shouldn't have worried about her. But I did.

I carved a hollow in both ends of a board, and wrapped a fifty-foot length of clothesline lengthwise around it, so that it could be unwound in a hurry, like an oversized trolling line.

In the first days of the new ice I would watch from the shore, sketching the flowing figure in charcoal but with my big string handy. I intended, in case of necessity, to hold on to the loose end and throw the stick to the swimming skater.

I never got to try that out, even though Fay often skated over ice that looked frighteningly thin to me. She did use the line once, though.

She took it along, one afternoon, on a little skating party with Irene, our baby-sitter, and Ham, who had just started kindergarten.

Fay skated out first to look over the lake. She saw that, some fifty feet out from shore, the ice took on a suspiciously dark color. She told the others to keep off that.

They had skated some distance along the firm white margin when they heard the loud whisper of blades behind them. Turning, they saw two young men skimming fast over the dark ice.

Fay raised her hand to wave them back, then realized that it was too late for that. The best chance now was that their speed would carry them over. She stood tense, watching.

There was the sound of breaking ice, then the tinkle of shards sliding across the surface. The man in the lead had disappeared.

He came up, swimming hard, weighed down with skates and sweaters. His companion hurried toward him, then stroked back as the hole sent a dark crack reaching out, wanting him too.

He shouted to the watching group to find a pole.

Fay was already coming. She stopped at a safe distance holding out the wrapped board. He skated toward her, grabbed it, and turned back, unwinding it.

That was a mistake. You should hold the end of the line and throw the wound-up board, not the loose rope. As he approached the hole it was already badly tangled.

He swung the end into the water. The swimmer gripped it, tried to haul himself out, failed, fell back, tried again. The man on the ice pulled hard, but his skates kept slipping. Fay could see that they were not going to make it.

She moved out, reached for a loop of the line. The man stepped toward her to hand it to her. She heard the ice groan between them.

"Watch it!" she warned. "Don't get too close."

He swung the loop to her. She heard Ham give a mournful cry. She turned, put the rope over her shoulder, dug the teeth of her figure skates into the ice and pulled.

They began to gain. The man at the other end was coming out of the water. He was holding to the rope with one hand now, lifting himself with the other. He got a knee on the surface.

The ice broke beneath him. He went down and under.

Irene was watching in an agony of anxiety and eagerness to help. She started forward.

"Keep back!" Fay shouted.

Her pull-partner looked at her in surprise. But she knew ice. One more person out there and they'd all be in the water.

Bending their backs to the rope, chopping and scraping with their skates, they got their man up again. Again the ice gave way under his weight.

Nobody was keeping track of how many times this action was repeated, nor of how long it took. It was a punishing, frightening struggle for the two above, with the sound of the ice continually cracking and breaking close behind them. Fay wondered, at each skate-push, whether this time she would break through.

At last, when they were all quite exhausted, they reached firm ice. One more slipping, straining effort and there he was on his hands and knees. He tried to get up, fell forward, rested his head on the ice. Then he struggled to his feet, took a few wobbly strokes and, gaining strength, skated to the landing. Fay had an extra overcoat in the car and offered it, but he wouldn't stop now for anything.

A few days later, when the lake had frozen hard, I stepped off the marks of the breakthrough. It covered a distance of 130 feet.

Fay told me that as she left the lake, she looked back at the long gash. A flock of snowbirds had settled beside it for a drink. It occurred to her that they'd have done the same if the rescue had failed. Nature neither loves nor hates us. It doesn't care.

Chapter 25

BEWARE THE ORINIAC

> The snow that falls hath not the strength
> to stop the oriniac, which is a mighty strong
> beast, much like a mule, having a tayle cut off
> 2 or 3 thumbes long, the foot cloven like a stagge.
> He has a muzzle mighty big. I have seen some that
> have nostrils so big that I put into it my two fists
> with ease.
>
> Pierre Esprit Radisson

It is the good, if unflattering, fortune of the human race that we don't smell or taste very good to our fellow predators. They may kill us because of fear, or outrage at our behavior, or just for the hell of it, but not usually for food. Not if they can find anything better.

I have known two people to be killed by bears in this area. Not much of a danger compared to real killers like automobiles and power sleds.

We have some fine big timberwolves that could do considerable damage to a man if they put their minds to it. But they are even less ambitious than bears. I never heard of anybody being attacked by wolves. Wild wolves anyway. Tame wolves can get just as vicious as dogs.

Oh, but there was that one case. The hunter who had scented himself up with doe juice to attract bucks. A wolf grabbed him by the arm. As soon as he realized what he'd gotten hold of, he let go and apologized. You could hardly blame him for that error.

Ernest Thompson Seton, the naturalist, tells of having been attacked by a lynx. Nobody else ever was, that I have heard of.

At least a hundred years ago the cougar was exterminated in Minnesota. All this time a few have been holding out in Manitoba. Now they are being seen and their tracks authenticated this side of the border. I guess there have been a few attacks on humans out in the western mountains. So far as I know they have never bothered anybody around here. Welcome back.

The easiest way to meet a really dangerous animal in the woods is to find a clearing, climb through a barbed wire fence, and find a friendly farm bull. That's how my brother arranged it.

The bull was pleased to make his acquaintance. He needed a romp. He pranced up to Lewis, put his head down, and pushed. Pushed some more. And moved faster, not hurting Lew much, but moving him right along. Lewis was hanging on to the horns, trying to keep away from them. He tripped over a stump elbow and went down.

Now the bull really began to have fun. He rolled and bounced Lew over the rooty ground of the pasture. Bunted him down every time he tried to get up.

He shoved him over the edge of a hill, going faster and getting friskier as the land sloped away. At the foot of this grade was the fence. With a final hook, the bull sent Lewis rolling under it. That spoiled the fun. The bull ran hopefully back and forth, snorting, looking for an opening in the fence, but finding none. Lew got up and went away quickly, battered and bloody but with no bones broken.

In earlier times a lot of settlers died that way. With artificial insemination there are not many bulls left in out-of-the-way stump lots. But tractors often roll over on hillsides and do a pretty good job at squashing their owners.

A moose—Radisson's *oriniac*—is nowhere near so dangerous. A farm bull may get rough at any time. The aboriginal bulls are almost never aggressive except during the fall mating season.

At that time an Indian can call them with a cone of birch bark. He puts the small end to the outside of his lips and talks moose through it. He double dares any bull in the country to come near his cow.

A rival bull may answer by bellowing back, splashing through water, splintering fallen timber, or just drifting silently toward the caller. Any moose that responds will come with his ears laid back, and the ruff over his hump standing up, looking for a fight. The hunter listens between calls, turns his head, watches sharp in all directions. He doesn't want to be taken by surprise.

At this season even an uninvited bull may make a pass at a man, usually a charge that stops short of actual contact. The trouble is that you don't know for sure just how serious he may be.

On a rocky Canadian hillside the mingled bones of a moose and a man were found. Beside them lay a rusty rifle. One shot had been fired through it and then it had jammed.

Early one morning in October, so early that it was still hardly more than night, Fay and I were waked by the sound of breaking brush. We had been sleeping in the open where a scattering of aspens and birches bordered a marsh. The sky was beginning to lighten, but the mist was so heavy that we could see only a few of the slender trees round us.

A cow moose came crashing out of the woods, straight at us. She must have caught our scent. She turned a little, passed close beside us, headed out over the muskeg, and faded into the fog. Another followed right in her tracks, and then a third.

By now we were sitting up in our blankets. Fay said afterwards that it was like sitting in a movie house and watching figures pass on the screen.

Right behind the cows came a bull. At the angle in the cows' trail he stopped, blew out his breath, took a good whiff. He turned, staring at us, looking enormous.

I reached for the gun, the old .22 that we had brought along for partridge. That was a reflex action. I hope that if the bull had come for us, I would have had sense enough not to sting him with that peanut bullet.

He didn't. He snorted, punched the ground once with a hoof, then turned and pounded off after the cows, sending gobs of mud flying as he hit the soft spots.

I stepped off the distance. The big cloven tracks were six paces from where we were lying.

This encounter could not be called a narrow escape, but the space was narrow.

The Anishinabeg used to hunt moose with .22 rifles when that was all they had. They would shoot one through the lungs and then follow him until he dropped, which might take a day or longer. But it's no moose gun.

We liked to sleep without a tent whenever the weather was clear, cool enough to discourage mosquitoes, and yet not fiercely freezing. It's good to look up at the stars and feel the evening breeze on your face.

On such a night as this, Fay was brought out of her sleep by little hands that gently stroked her hair. She twisted around on an elbow and found herself face to face with a porcupine. Fearing a quillful tail-slap, she called me.

I thought that she must have dreamed a porky, and said so. But I got out of my blanket, and there he was. I followed him as he fell back and up a tree. If it's possible to fall up.

The fretful porpentine will sometimes come into camp at night to clean up leftover food or to gnaw a sweat-salted paddle shaft.

This one hadn't been grazing on Fay's hair. He must have been just playing with it, or admiring it.

By this time you may be feeling some disappointment that, in each of these cases, the wild animal got close and then just went away without doing anything wild. Well, I warned you that I was only going to tell what happened, and that's the way almost all these encounters turn out. Domestic animals—dogs, horses, and bulls—do plenty of damage to people. But in any conflict between man and beast in the wilderness it's usually the beast that gets hurt. The animals seem to understand that and to act accordingly.

But now I will tell you about a varmint that, although not so big as a moose nor so well protected as a porcupine, and although outnumbered two to one, still managed to leave his mark on me.

I was walking over a strip of plowed land separated from the barnyard by a six-foot fence. Mike was on pest patrol, sniffing around the barn.

Suddenly he snapped into action. He had started a big one. The rat scooted through the fence and headed for the woods behind me. The dog tore for the gate fifty yards away.

Rats are bad on a farm. They eat a lot of grain and are especially fond of eggs and small birds. I didn't want this one to get away.

I jumped to head him off, arms outstretched. On flat ground he would have flashed past me, but the furrows slowed him. He retreated a little, ran to one side, tried again. I stepped in front of him, shooing him back. Out of the corner of my eye I saw Mike round the gate post.

The rat saw him too and made a determined end run. Again I blocked him. He hesitated, looked at the fast-approaching dog, then made a dash under my arm.

I knew better than to grab him. I swung at him in an openhanded scoop that flung him sailing into the dog's path. A quick motion. I touched him for only a fraction of a second, but in that time he got in a slashing bite.

Then Mike had him, gave him an expert shake that sent him flying again. He came down a dead rat.

My hand was bleeding nicely but I had to admire this little demonstration of the cool judgment that animals show in an emergency. The dog and the rat had each played the game out the very best they could. The rat had tried to avoid me. When that was no longer possible, he took his last fighting chance.

Another encounter was with a still smaller adversary.

After we had shivered through the first winter in our little house in the woods, we decided to put a basement under it. I dug the excavation out with pick and shovel. The hardpan got so hard that I didn't go down as deep as I should have. When I go into the basement I have to stoop so as not to bump my head.

With Hilmer's help I built board forms and poured in concrete, along with many stones to reduce the amount of cement needed. I'd never done any of this kind of work, but I read the skimpy written instructions available. I claim I didn't do so badly. The walls have lasted all these years. But I can't say that they are either straight or waterproof. There is always a small puddle in the middle of the floor.

A colony of little spotted salamanders took up residence on the shores of this body of water. They never did us any harm, so we didn't bother them. But they never quite trusted us.

The biggest buck lizard was about four inches long. Sometimes, when we stood looking down at him, he turned defiant. Instead of joining his women and children in the scramble for cover he rared back on straightened front legs, jaws spread menacingly, ready to charge.

The posture was always good for a laugh from whichever one of us was being threatened. Fay said, "He thinks he's a dinosaur." I suppose that he'd later tell the others how he'd driven off the intruder.

Old age and minding your own business are not sure defenses against animal attack. On an evening not long ago, when I was sitting peacefully barefoot at my desk, I felt a stinging pain in a toe. No cause in sight. I thought that it must have been a needle in the carpet but could find none. The next night I felt it again. This time a field mouse was hanging to the toe. I shook it off and grabbed the

nearest weapon, a yardstick, to defend myself, but the mouse was gone.

Mauled by a mouse. This one must have been a real man-eater. It was clear that if I didn't stop him he would devour me completely, taking a bite each night until there would be nothing left. I put out a trap and caught him.

I called a doctor. Did he want the mouse for testing? Should I be inoculated for rabies? No. He wasn't worried. But then it wasn't his toe.

He was right, though. No rabies.

Chapter 26

THE ONCE AND FUTURE QUEEN

> Thus the birch canoe was builded
> And the forest's life was in it . . . .
> Longfellow

"Below that bluff across the bay. No, not there. Look where I'm pointing. The bow'n arrers are back. Let's you and me go over there tonight, kid, and see what we can get for a half a pint of moonshine."

I found a slender column of smoke and followed it down to three brown domes. Wigwams. They hadn't been there in the morning.

Vic, a friendly logger, and I, an interested young visitor, rowed across the water that evening. We were welcomed with customary Anishinabe hospitality. The half-pint was welcomed too, but failed to accomplish the desired results.

The only sound on the return trip was the squeak of the oarlocks. Vic, steering from the stern, said nothing until I had stepped ashore and had pulled the prow up the beach below the bunk house.

"God damned squaws! Won't do nothing no more without

you've got cash money. Getting to be just as mean as white women.

"But say, wasn't that a pretty little canoe. Couldn't have been more than eight feet long, and yet everything about it just right. I've got to have it."

Vic had fallen in love, but not with a woman.

After payday at the logging camp and a successful poker game he rowed back and made an offer. Sensing his infatuation, the wily savages took him for everything but his scalp. He paid them thirty dollars of his own money and ten pounds of sugar that he had obtained, in some way, from the cook shanty.

By then, I had left the camp for school. The next time I came back Vic showed me his little sweetheart and generously offered to let me take her out. But he warned me that she was as tricky as she was beautiful.

I recognized that as an understatement. Stability in a canoe demands some length. The smallest one that I had used up to then had been almost twice as long as this.

And she had a reputation. When I carried her down to the water I found an expectant audience of lumberjacks assembled on the dock. I felt like a rodeo rider waiting in the chute on some notorious bull or mustang.

I stepped in cautiously, knelt in the bottom, paddled a few prudent strokes, tipped gracefully to port, corrected the tilt firmly, and capsized to starboard.

The next try took me a little farther but ended in the same way. After a few more attempts I managed to stay right side up for a while. Eventually I was able to paddle around quite freely as long as the lake was calm and my hair was parted in the middle.

The little canoe had been shaped and crafted for a serious purpose. Those old-time Anishinabeg had a great sense of humor, but it did not extend to building a boat just for a practical joke. This was a special-purpose hunting canoe, light enough to be carried through brush and over rough country to some distant water. A single paddle stroke, properly delivered, could swing into a reverse turn. It had been designed for an expert, not for a clumsy white man. Using it added to my appreciation of the birch canoe and its inventors and builders.

Nobody knows when it first happened, but it was a long time ago that somebody used the long, tough roots of the tamarack to bind together a cedar frame, covered it with birch bark, caulked it with a mixture of spruce gum, bear's grease and charcoal, carried it to the water, and eased himself down into it. Those materials don't wait around for the archeologist as stone, metal, and pottery do. But certainly for centuries, and perhaps for millennia, this was the only practical means of transportation over the unfrozen waterways of the great American forest.

Down through the years, a superbly functional form was developed. No modern designer has been able to improve it. Canoes built today in factories vary in shape, but every one of them that is useful for travel is a pretty close repetition of some Indian model.

The European explorers who first came here were experienced boatmen, but the bark canoe amazed them with its lightness, shallow draft, and cargo capacity. In case of damage, repair materials were everywhere. A man or woman could lift even a fairly big canoe, shoulder it, and carry it over the trail from one watercourse to another. An early observer called it the queen of the lakes and rivers.

Other features of the new continent did not impress our forefathers so favorably. This should not surprise us, in view of the Puritan belief that Satan dwelled in nature. The chronicler of Plymouth Colony wrote of the "hideous and desolate wilderness." Americans and Canadians ever since have felt the need to subdue and dominate the forest, not only by cutting its trees and damming its rivers, but also, wherever possible, by changing its primitive character.

They are comforted by the sounds and smells of civilization as much as by its conveniences. This would seem to be an important factor in the popularity of the outboard motor.

Those of us who value solitude have found that we cannot escape these loud, extravagant, undependable, stinking, game-scaring, polluting and fattening contrivances until we have put at least one long portage behind us, and that we'd better not really relax until we've passed over several. So we may be willing to accept, or beg, or even hire a tow from one of the filthy things to speed us through their noise and exhaust belt. Then we pay or thank the motorman and carry our canoe over the silent trail, not hoping that the machine will break down or run out of gas on the return trip, but serene in the knowledge of our own superiority.

Fortunately, from our point of view, the small outboard on a portageable canoe has not proved efficient for most wilderness travel. We see such combinations in the back country occasionally. They pass us on open water, but we get ahead when it comes time for the boat to ride the people. Over a period of days on a route that has an average proportion of portaging, we will leave them behind. They can't escape the inexorable fact that five gallons of gasoline weighs forty pounds. A man really has to love the pop of the pistons and the smell of exhaust to lug one of those outfits over the timber-tangled portages of the Canadian shield.

An even worse drawback is the risk of taking a light motorized canoe—light enough for portaging—down rapids or across windy lakes. If the engine conks out in white water the crew may be in trouble. The paddled canoe passes safely over waves that would leave the square-stern plus outboard bobbing, bow up, like a fishing float.

But closer to road-access points and on the expanses of water that extend out from them, the heavy boat with high horsepower outboard is supreme. They get the speedy sports where they want to be taken: out to the fishing and hunting grounds in the morning and back to the beer and television at night. No need to sleep in the hideous wilderness in danger of attack by owls and porcupines.

Nobody could call such a boat a queen, but I can't deny that these broad-bottomed, unflippable dames are safe. You can climb all around one of them, or stumble across her, or lean out over the gunwale without seriously disturbing her aplomb.

Maybe it's being accustomed to this extreme solidity that has made many people afraid of canoes. They really aren't that tippy, if you stay out of birch bark midgets. You soon get used to balancing a canoe just as you do a bicycle, so that it becomes difficult to capsize: it takes a real effort.

Indians have been just as susceptible as whites to the prestige of the machine. Many of them have lost the traditional skill and confidence in canoes. To see an Anishinabe worried about stepping into a canoe is like watching a Sioux hesitate to mount a horse. Neither sight is unusual when city Indians come back to the reservation.

◌₃℞

The wind was shaking the jackpines above us as my wife, my son, and I passed through a bay of Lac Seul and headed out through a narrows into the main body of the lake. We knew that we'd be in for some heavy paddling but were not worried about being able to get through it.

A group of Indians were watching us from where their boats were beached. One of them ran out on a point that extended into the channel. He was shouting, but his words were blown away. As we passed he held out his closed fists, one over the other, then reversed their positions in a quick motion. You didn't have to know sign language to get the message.

It was a responsible warning. Those waves would have been too much for their square sterns, weighted down with motors, but they would be no danger to us. I waved my thanks and we kept going.

As we came out of the narrows into the wind I could remember a stormier stretch of water on another big lake. We Whites were the windbound party then, standing on a high rock with the surf crashing beneath us. Sometimes it sprayed over us but we held our place there, watching a dark spot in the whitecaps gradually enlarge into a bark canoe. It would appear on a rising crest, then dip out of sight in a trough. As it approached we could see that it was manned (if that is the proper term) by two calm little Indian girls.

That's how much times have changed during my lifetime.

They're still changing. During the past fifteen years a reverse trend to the hand-paddled canoe has been noticeable, especially for long trips into wilderness areas. Some routes over back country rivers and chains of lakes that had been abandoned by power boaters of both races are being reopened by paddlers. But great expanses of territory once used by canoeists remain empty.

Our short, wild era of the prodigal expenditure of earth's resources seems to be drawing to a close. As gasoline prices rise and the craze for motorized toys wanes, more people are becoming familiar with the advantages of the hand-powered canoe. The queen may reign again.

Chapter 27

RIDING THE TURTLE

> Do you know the blackened timber . . . do you know
>   the racing stream
> With the raw, right-angled log jamb at the end;
> And the bar of sun-warmed shingle where a man
>   bask and dream,
> To the click of shod canoe-poles round the bend . . . .
>
> Kipling

The Indians of my younger days were the finest canoe-people that I have ever seen. They used a short, quick stroke, applying the greatest muscular effort at exactly the point that would produce the maximum forward impetus. With time out for tea at noon they kept the pace all day.

They portaged quietly. Nobody gave orders, but everybody knew what to do. The men and women walked swiftly, or trotted, under heavy burdens. Even the toddlers carried something.

It was a pleasure to see them work a canoe upstream in fast

water. Every person except those tied in the cradle boards would be pushing on poles.

Since then, canoeing has changed. Shooting rapids has become an organized sport. Not just in the north country, but anywhere a stretch of rocky downhill water remains undammed.

Books are written about how to run rapids, and the technique is taught in canoe schools. Rivers are mapped and graded, according to speed and risk, on a scale of 1–6.

Canoes designed and reinforced for this special purpose are built of light, strong, modern materials. Their occupants are protected, in case of upset, by wet suits, inflated jackets, and helmets like those of football players.

Many of the people who specialize in this sport are experts, better than I ever was. But I don't think that even their champions would have been a match for the woods Indians.

These were the Crees and those Northern Anishinabeg who lived on their own, beyond the reservations or any other form of white control or assistance. They were accustomed to risking their lives in rapids, just as they did on windy lakes or half-frozen ice, not for any thrill, but because they had to.

Each of the tasks of their work-year—making maple sugar, picking berries, gathering wild rice, fishing, trapping, shooting or snaring meat—had to be carried out at the right time and place. There was cruelly little margin for error or delay.

So a family or a group of families moving from a fishing camp to the rice lakes might deliberately accept a moderate risk in running rapids rather than portage around them, because the time spent in the carries would result in a smaller harvest and possible death by starvation in the snowbound woods.

Every such risk was carefully calculated. These people knew each stretch of rapids, and how each varied in depth and speed from day to day and hour to hour depending on rainfall in the high country. A mile upstream they would be reading the river by the condition of the banks, the color of the water, the behavior of ducks and shorebirds.

As they approached the chute the paddles would stop. The canoes would glide silently but with increasing speed in the growing pull of the current. A man would rise to his feet, steering with the paddle in one hand, looking down at the rock-torn river.

He was studying the interweaving of surface currents, listening to the sound of the rapids, and straining to hear, above that growing roar, the surge of water pouring over some remembered ledge. He might be observing a mist that drifted up behind a screen of trees and warned him of a particular danger. Or maybe he could sense, through the soles of his moccasins, a change in the pull of the river that might reveal what lay ahead—as the steersman of a Polynesian catamaran was able to feel the change in motion that resulted from an island out of sight over the Pacific horizon, so that, if food or water was running low, he might turn the craft and home in on that island, following the break in wave action all the way to its source.

The river people sat relaxed but ready, their paddles dripping. If the leading canoe turned toward the portage, the others followed. Or else, spaced out in single file, they moved after it into the opening vee of the channel. There was no discussion. It was seldom that the choice proved wrong.

Nobody of either race is that good at reading white water now. There is no longer the grim inspiration of hunger.

When I was a child, a grown-up cousin showed me how to use pole and paddle in the rapids of the Brule River in Wisconsin. It was a good place to learn.

The big rivers of the North are less forgiving. In one of those the canoe of another cousin, my instructor's brother, was turned into rags and broken boards. He made it out of the river alive and back to civilization on foot. His experience should have been a warning to me, and it was, for a while.

But a voyager is drawn into rapids by more than just the current. They exert an intoxicating, habit-forming appeal. Something says, "Don't haul the canoe and all this cargo over that rocky, crooked, buggy old portage. Take a chance. You never died yet, so you probably won't this time."

Bending Lake was one of those wonderful Canadian places: clear water, set deep in forested hills and undefiled by cabins, camp sites or other evidence of the dirty human race.

We had been working hard through several days of wind and rain, paddling across stormy lakes, pushing and chopping through overgrown trails. Now in clear weather, we took a rest on a long point of sand. We swam, painted, slept in the sun, and ate the big walleyes that Ham, then sixteen, brought up out of the lake.

The next wavy line on our map was marked *Turtle R.* We didn't know it, but this was an *R.* with a reputation. Ham was about to get a liberal education in rapids. His parents, too, would pick up a few pointers on sliding down steep water.

As we paddled south, the shores of the lake gradually converged and seemed to end, ahead, in a level line across the water. It was a drop-off into fast rapids. Ham wanted to run them but was overruled. We sweat-portaged up a rock ledge and down its slippery opposite side.

More rapids came soon. Standing up in the canoe, I couldn't see the end of them.

"Seems that we'll be doing more carrying than riding on this river. But let's take a look first."

We walked down the bank, stepping down sometimes and out over the stones, wading or jumping between them or climbing over driftwood to far-out rocks. From these vantage points, Fay and I picked out a likely ladder of vees and chutes that seemed to form a

continuous and reasonably safe track of water between the boulders and around the ledges. We left Ham at the foot of the rapids, walked back to the canoe, pushed off and paddled into the main stream.

The sensations were familiar, but more intense than we had felt before: the scary thrill of passing the point of no return, of feeling the current take its powerful grip on the canoe, of handing ourselves over to the wild spirits of this unknown water.

Swiftly increasing speed. Boulders flashed by, and white hills of foam. Tall waves of rushing water stood still or only wavered a little where they were flung up by deep, invisible rocks. Fast, too fast, but we must not brake the speed with our paddles.

Must rather dig them in, adding our small push to the strength of the river. We couldn't just allow ourselves to be carried by the current. We had to move faster than the water was moving. Only in this way could we control direction, make the sharp turns that were needed.

Fay, as bow man, steered through the rough places. From her position she could see approaching under-water hazards before I could. She pried or pulled the bow sharply right or left to miss them. My job was to follow, matching her strokes, keeping the boat headed downstream instead of crossways. When we came into smooth stretches I took over the steering again.

We worked with closed mouths. Shouted warnings would have been a waste of breath in the roar of the water. She was telling me with her actions what she saw. I managed the stern accordingly.

A long distance of river went by in a short time. The rapids ended in patterns of white froth swirling across a dark pool. We swung in to pick up the kid.

This strategy of walking over the portage while the old folks took the fun ride did not appeal to him. He had quite a lot to say about it in the little time before the next rapid.

This one didn't look so tough. We ran it with Ham in the bow and Fay coaching into his ear from a sitting position on the tent roll just behind him. It went well, and we did several more the same way.

We heard a sound ahead that grew beyond the roar of rapids. A waterfall. The portage around it was all downhill. We carried canoe and packs down the steep trail and found a party of Indians at the landing.

Their canoes were factory-built instead of birch bark. They were launching and loading them as efficiently as ever, but the flashing paddle skill was no longer evident.

As we set our canoe in beside theirs they were attaching outboard motors and handing down cans of gasoline. That takes time, and we all pushed off together.

They sped ahead but stopped at the next portage. They had to, of course. We landed too, checked the rapid on foot, found it not especially long or steep. We ran it with ease. It would have been impossible for the Indian party, with all that weight of fuel and hardware.

A person becomes addicted to white water. Ham would cock his head, listen intently, then let out a whoop of joy. He'd heard the song of the next rapid. We'd all perk up.

It had been our practice to walk the longer rapids, to make sure of a plausible path all the way. But this preliminary scrambling over rocks and washed-up timber was getting tiresome. We cut our inspection down to just an over-the-bow appraisal. Where the rapids extended out of sight, two of us would wait in the canoe to give the third person time to walk over the portage. That lightened the load and provided a watcher at the foot of the rapid in case of trouble.

Sluing down one of these long stretches, Ham and I came around a bend into a narrowing gorge. As the rock walls converged, the river took on more speed. I wished that we had checked this one, but it was too late to turn back and there was no place to stop here.

We dropped to our knees, swerving the canoe to one side and the other, trying to avoid the rocks, standing waves, and white fountains. But not entirely succeeding. Those high places were spilling too much water in over the side.

A shock from below sent me sprawling forward across the thwart. The canoe was hanging on a rock, caught at the end of a long groove in the aluminum hull. We got back into position and pushed down on the stone with our paddles.

With that boost, the river tore us loose and swept us on. Now we could hear the growing roar of falling water.

Blurred towers of stone turned us to the right and then to the left. At that second bend the bow dropped. The canoe tilted forward. I lost sight of Ham's back as he disappeared in a surge of spray. For the fraction of a second I was alone. Then I followed him down into the seething whiteness.

We had been poured over a waterfall. Somehow we hit the lower level right side up and not on rock. We had been shaken dizzy and the battered boat was almost full of water. We were still afloat.

Ham looked back at me, smiling a little through the trickles running down his face.

Cautiously we maneuvered the sloshing, tipsy craft across the river to the rock where our wife and mother was standing, ready to come in if she should be needed.

We had completed the white water course and had passed our final examination. With a low grade, to be sure, and by luck rather than by knowledge. But we hadn't quite flunked out, and we had learned our lesson. We wouldn't run out-of-sight rapids again without full-length inspection.

We laid over on a lakelike opening to hang our watersoaked gear in the sun and to club the long dent out of the canoe with a stump mallet. That night our blankets were not very dry, but we slept well.

Next morning we heard the sound of outboards. The Indians were coming. One of them cut off his motor and called over the water.

"Where did you get by us? You must have run them all." He frowned, shook his head, and spun the motor.

Chapter 28

SEAS AND SHORES OF 'TSCHGUMI

> Though its waters are fresh and crystal,
> Lake Superior is a sea. It is cold in mid-
> summer as the Atlantic. It is wild, masterful
> and dread as the Black Sea.
>
> George Grant

"Sacred Blue! It's just fresh water!"

When the first French explorer knelt and scooped up a cupped handful of this lake he was disappointed not to taste salt. He hoped that he had discovered the northwest passage. He wanted this to be a bay of the Pacific. And it does look like an ocean. The curve of the horizon is all you can see out there.

This is the largest body of fresh water in the world: 380 miles long and 160 wide. Because of its reefs, dense fogs, quick-shifting winds and sudden storms, many experienced seamen consider it also the most dangerous body of water, fresh or salt. In earlier years, when ore shipping extended into the gale season of early winter, resignations sometimes became epidemic among the crews. The larger ships of recent times are giving men more confidence.

Old sailors say that we can't yet be certain that this trust is justified. Iron ore makes a heavy cargo. When a ship loaded with ore strikes a reef, or when wave action loosens its rivets or tears away its hatch covers, it may plunge suddenly to the bottom.

Sailor talk doesn't provide much encouragement for beginners. They are told that, here on Lake Siberia, life jackets are provided only to help the coast guard tidy up after a wreck and balance its books.

Another saying is that Lake Superior never gives up its dead. There are exceptions, but temperatures in the depths may be too low to allow a body to decompose, so that no gas is generated to float it to the surface. Salvage divers report that the folks they meet aboard ships down there look pretty good, considering.

Well, enough of bodies and boogey men. I open this chapter with such macabre references to make it clear that this is not a good place for inexperienced or overly-brave people in any kind of a boat. I wouldn't want my enthusiasm for canoeing on 'Tschgumi to entice anybody out there who hasn't first become proficient on lesser lakes. And he should still be cautious.

The northern coast is rock, with an occasional beach of sand, pebbles, or rounded stones. A highway defaces the Minnesota shore but bends away from the lake at the Ontario border. Here, hills come down to the water and out into it, ending in peninsulas, chains of islands, and scattered, solitary rocks.

This steep terrain, continuing along most of the Canadian coast, is not easily converted to a shoreline drive. The highway borders the lake in only a few short stretches between Grand Portage, Minnesota, and Marathon, Ontario. There, both road and railway let go of the lake entirely and swing inland, leaving 150 miles of silent and austerely beautiful coast east to Michicipoten Bay. Long may it stay that way!

At several points in Minnesota, and many in Ontario, walls of vertical rock, locally called palisades, rise above the lake. Some of these are over 200 feet high and extend for miles along the shore.

Grinding into these precipices with masses of storm-rolled stones, the lake has carved out caves. Some of these run far back under the forest and may emerge at another entrance. In calm weather we explored them, Fay boldly, I with some fear. I looked down at the giant slabs of rock below us, and then up at others that

still hung from the ceiling, wondering when these might drop off. I figured that nothing like that would happen except during a storm. But I still didn't feel comfortable while we were under those dangling boulders.

At one time or another Fay and I have paddled along most of this coast. We didn't see canoes here, either on the water or ashore. Motor boats were numerous around the city harbors, but those that go far out into the lake are not adapted to landing on this kind of shore. Most of them return to their home ports at night.

But it is a lovely place for canoe camping, and more accessible than any other solitary shoreline. When you have put in at Grand Portage, it only takes an hour or two or three—depending on the wind--to cross the Bay of Spearing by Torchlight and enter the Susie islands. Here you are already in primitive country. You may meet a fishing boat or see the line of smoke hanging above a distant steamer. But the lichens, moss, and runty, storm-twisted little trees are undisturbed by campsites.

The same is true when you enter the lake at most places on the Canadian side. As soon as you pass the first headland you have escaped from the crowds, noises, and toxic fumes of progress.

In calm weather the lake is so clear that, looking down from your canoe, you feel that you are floating on air. Not much grows or blooms to cloud that cold, submarine landscape. You watch your shadow move in zigzag jumps across ledges and boulders. That one looks too close. You push your paddle down at it, touch nothing.

When the wind blows, 'Tschgumi sorts his stones. He sifts sand into the deep indentations and river mouths, pours pebbles into more open bays, and piles up various larger sizes along certain shores selected according to curves and currents.

He's not quiet about this work. As you walk along a terrace of pumpkin-sized cobblestones during a storm you can hear others clicking like dice under the water. Even on a calm night the water sighs mournfully along a pebble beach as each long, slow swell runs out its length and dies among the little stones.

Along its shallow southern edge, the lake will sometimes hurl big rocks across a beach and into the trees. These can be so heavy that they move with the deadly momentum of spent cannon balls. Even as they slow down you'd better keep out of their way.

The most violent and relentless storms come from the Northeast, but these usually give warning. The fishermen of the north shore receive the signals, take their nets up and get off the lake. More dangerous is the sudden northwest wind. This can build up to great force behind the shelter of the shore range, then shift a little, find a gap in the ridges, and sweep a boat out into the lake.

There is a comforting saying that the farther you are blown from one shore the closer you are to the other. But who wants to ride to Michigan that way?

Duluth, the air-conditioned city, was undergoing a heat wave. Fay and I had driven up to the Canadian side in our shirt sleeves, with all the windows open and still hot. We put our canoe in at Jarvis Bay and immediately were comfortably cool. At Mink Island we picked out a dense thicket to camp in. By that time we were looking for shelter rather than breeze.

While supper was cooking we put on parkas and spread our hands to the fire. Later we piled on driftwood to warm the open tent, changed to woolen underwear, crawled into goose-down sleeping bags, and pulled the hoods up around our heads.

When we got home we learned that everybody else in the United States and Canada had been lying sweatily awake that night with sheets and blankets thrown off.

In later years I found it impossible to get my pupils to bring warm clothes when we were leaving a sweltering city for landscape work on the shore. As the afternoon aged and cooled, the class members would one by one be frozen out.

I got to keeping a bundle of paint-smeared old jackets in the back of the truck. The joy with which these were accepted, even by stylish ladies, was gratifying. No sacrifice is too great to make for art. For anybody who really wanted to finish her painting, looking a little messy was better than shivering.

But days can be hot in a canoe floating between the summer sun and its reflection in the lake. Sometimes, when the air is still and rain clouds hang heavy, an evening may be warm and muggy. But you have to be ready for cold nights at any season. Since portages are seldom necessary on the big lake, we came to indulge in such luxuries as heavy clothing, blowbeds, and warm sleeping bags here, at a time when we were still going light on inland travels.

Starting out along an isolated coast we would be careful to check each landmark against the map. If you once lose track of your location along the Canadian shore you may not find it again until somebody comes along and straightens you out. That may not be for quite a while.

Even the large scale government maps don't show all the small islands. You may pass through a cluster of tiny islets, none of them big enough to make the map, and yet adding up to quite an expanse of rock.

In windy weather I watched the shoreline, noting bays, creeks, coves, islands, and other irregularities that might give protection for

an emergency landing. I would hold each such potential haven in mind until we came to the next one. Thus we could always turn, if we had to, and head for the nearest exit.

The sun had gone down on a cold September evening, the wind was piling surf against the cliffs to the North, and we were looking for a place to get ashore. I had tucked the map into the binding of the pack in front of me to keep it from blowing away. Leaning forward over it I could just make out the faint blue line of a river.

As I looked up at the shore, there it was, a narrow gap shining out of the dark mass of spruce and granite. We swung in, riding the front of the wave, watching for any rocks that might break the gleaming surface of the trough that rolled ahead of us. Then sud--denly we were coasting calmly under the protection of overhanging stone.

A different kind of camp site is needed on those still nights when heat lightning flares over the lake, thunder rolls in the distance, and the mosquitoes waiting along the shore are dense enough to form a visible cloud.

It was on that kind of a night that Fay and I paddled along the Canadian shore in our new aluminum canoe. We wanted the most exposed place that we could find, to catch any feeble breeze that might come wandering over the water. This turned out to be on a granite ridge, the backbone of an island.

We tied our tent between two dwarfed and distorted jackpines whose enterprising roots had managed to find enough moss and dirt to allow life and a little growth. I carried the canoe up close to camp, turned it bottom up so that it would not be filled by the approaching rain, and laid a drift log across it to keep it from getting restless if a wind should come up. That would have been good enough for a wood-and-canvas canoe.

The tin boat proved lighter and more lively. I waked in the night and listened comfortably to the drum song of rain on our wind-tightened tent. Then there was another sound, the ring of metal on stone. Instantly I became a barefoot ballerino, following the dance of the canoe across the rock. I caught it just before it took the final dive off the end of the island. After that we tethered it every night like a skittish horse.

Our tent stayed put that night. It wasn't going to uproot the jackpines and fly away with them. But on bare rock islands where there were no trees we had to set it up with driftwood poles. Then we guyed it tight with lines to whatever bushes might be growing in

crevices in the rock, or to substantial stones. I used to seek out a big forked log from the driftwood among the shore rocks and have it ready to brace the tent against whatever direction a wind might blow in from.

Another consideration in choosing a camping place on a big lake is the risk of being locked in by wind. We got good at unloading in heavy waves, but we never did figure out a way to load and push off in them. Even on the mildest evening, we tried to find a shore-shape that would provide some sheltered water no matter which way the wind might be blowing in the morning.

A tight cove or river-mouth was just right, but not always there when it was needed. Our second choice was an island or narrow point where we could carry across to the lee shore in case the waves should be plastering our side in the morning.

Being windbound needn't be so bad. When it happens on 'Tschgumi you know that you're not going anywhere until the storm lets up tonight or tomorrow or next week. That gives complete freedom to sleep, read or stroll in the woods. Relaxation here can be more complete than at home, where conscience may nag about neglected duties. The camper who paces back and forth, looking anxiously at the sky and cursing the weather, is losing out on one of the good experiences of canoe travel.

In my opinion a canoe, thoughtfully loaded, properly handled, and discreetly navigated, is safer on Lake Superior than any other small craft.

I have been terrified as a passenger on a large power boat as it bounced and battered its way through rough weather. I have looked back from the cabin of such a boat at our canoe, lashed upside down across the hull, and wondered whether we would be able to cut it loose and make our getaway if the ship should be overwhelmed.

It seems so much easier and safer just to ride over big waves than to blast through them. You are not going to develop engine trouble in a canoe, or run out of gas. If you are alert you can find a place to get ashore on almost any coast.

Fay and I have had enough confidence to take first our children and later our grandchildren on many canoe trips over all kinds of water, including Lake Superior's south shore and along the more moderate stretches of the north shore. I've sometimes thought, when the water riffled up a bit, how embarrassing it would be to have to tell a daughter or a daughter-in-law, "We had a nice trip but we lost little so-and-so." I'm afraid they wouldn't have liked it. But, so far, we've never drowned a kid.

Chapter 29

THE WANDERING HILLS

> A very little wind on these broad lakes raises a sea which will swamp a canoe. Looking off from the lee shore the surface may appear to be very little agitated, almost smooth a mile distant, or if you see a few white crests they may appear nearly level with the rest of the lake: but when you get out so far you may find quite a sea running. Erelong, before you think of it, a wave will gently creep up the side of your canoe and fill your lap, like a monster deliberately covering you with slime before it swallows you, or it will strike the canoe violently and break into it.
>
> Thoreau

From the shore, waves look alike. When you get out amongst them you quickly learn how much they differ in behavior as well as in size.

Some are legendary. Lake Superior sailors fear the Three Sisters, a trio of killer waves that stagger a ship and then sink it. We

never met those deadly witches. But I have seen monsters come, riding high above all their comrades.

Searching for landmarks along a distant shore and looking for the upshoot that shows a reef ahead, I have sometimes neglected the outward view. Fay would assume that I must be preparing to meet some advancing mountain. Then, suddenly, she would know that I hadn't seen it.

"Watch it!"

As its foothills began to lift us, I would swing the canoe to angle into the wind. If the crest was white above us I would lean out above the opposite gunwale, careening the boat so far over that we would almost ship water on the lee side. As the crest passed under us I would bear down on its surface with my paddle, shoving my weight back on center or beyond to right the canoe.

Rocking the boat like this to ward off a threatening wave is standard practice in stormy weather and is not so risky as it may sound. But it does call for a bow man who knows her business. She must stay on center and keep paddling, no matter how alarming the sideways slant of the hull. If she were to obey the natural impulse to counterbalance the tilt by shifting her weight, the canoe might swamp or capsize.

Along the Canadian coastline, one tempting shortcut after another offers itself. A headland appears in the distance. Shall we save miles by taking a course toward it or shall we play it safe by following the long curve of the shore?

Having taken a little chance on one of these crossings, we found that we had made the wrong guess. We were putting all the strength we had into our paddles, but the cape that had beckoned us wasn't getting closer.

At right angles to our course I could see a gray cliff rising above a dark fringe of spruce. The waves and froth-trails driven past us by the offshore wind gave the feeling that we were making pretty good headway. But when I looked again, after what seemed like a lot of heavy paddling, the stone was ahead of our right angle instead of behind it. For all our effort, we had been shoved backwards. Backwards and out.

In such a case there is nothing to do but push harder. When the realization gets through that the alternative is the open lake, it's surprising how much additional energy can be shoveled up. We came abreast of the cliff again. Inch by inch we passed it. The point began to get closer. In its shelter, the wind reluctantly relented. At last we were moving easily in quiet water.

I was tasting copper by that time and wondering whether my heart would take it. When we came ashore it took Fay a few minutes to open her hands enough to let go of the paddle.

After one more such worrisome experience we began to wonder what we would do if, some day, we should not be so lucky.

Our aluminum canoe had airtight bulkheads bow and stern. It would float even when swamped, and would hold our heads above water as long as we hung low beside it. That was fine for a warmer lake, but not good enough on 'Tschgumi. And as soon as we tried, in experimental spills, to hoist ourselves out of the water, either onto or into the canoe, it would revolve, dumping us back into the lake.

With practice, it's possible to empty a flooded canoe in deep water and climb into it. The instructor demonstrates this technique in some summer camps. The kids could memorize a lot of Latin verbs in the time it takes to master this stunt, and one achievement would do them just as much good as the other so far as canoe safety is concerned. Because this trick can't be done in rough weather, and that's when it would be needed.

The problem was how to convert a canoe full of water into a raft, using articles that would be in it on a cruise. Talking this over we decided that the air mattresses offered possibilities. We used the kind with a big open stem that makes inflating by mouth easy.

Working in comfortable onshore waves we lashed the paddles crossways of the swamped hull, partly inflated the air mattresses, rolled and bound them into cylinders, blew them up harder, and tied one end of each under the projecting paddles. Then we climbed aboard.

There was a tendency, as the raft tipped to one side or the other, for the submerged blowbed-pontoon to buckle upwards at its center. We fixed that with a couple of birch poles, trimmed smooth. Each of these was tied in the center of a rolled mattress.

This combination worked. We assembled it after a practice swamping in a heavy sea, and got our bodies (but not our legs) out of the water. We could even paddle it.

It took time, though, to do all that puffing and binding. This was in the comparatively warm water of an onshore wind. Would hands and fingers continue to function that long at the temperatures of the open lake?

I don't know. We never had to assemble our life raft in an emergency. Younger people may want to carry the experiment further.

We worked out another method that didn't require performance in the water. Bedding and extra clothes in watertight plastic bags were placed in the back of each pack: that is, on the flat side that is carried next to the shoulders. Such soft things belong there anyway for comfort in portaging. We put food and other heavies, also in plastic, in the front of the packs. We laid the packs flat in the canoe, heavy sides down, bedding and clothing up. We inflated the air mattresses at the start of the voyage, and didn't let the air out until we got back, except in case of a portage. (Even on 'Tschgumi you sometimes have to carry across a point or island to launch on its sheltered side.)

Each morning we wedged the beds lengthwise of the hull over the packs and under the thwarts, overlapping them at the center,

with a tarp over them. We pushed three poles lengthwise between the canvas and the thwarts to keep the mattresses from humping up and escaping in an upset.

We logged a lot of miles thus loaded, but, fortunately or unfortunately, did not swamp or capsize. So again I am unable to report results in an emergency. If the wind were to carry me out into the lake, though, and roll me over, I'd be glad to have that added buoyancy on the top of the load. And if I were then to drift up on some remote beach, I'd be thankful for food, dry clothing and blankets all lodged tight in the hull.

The crew of the wrecked Canadian ship Kamloops reached Isle Royale, but they all died there of cold and hunger. There have been, on this lake, many other deaths of shipwreck survivors that could have been avoided if there had been supplies and blankets.

A small but comforting piece of equipment was a foot-pump, a rubber bulb with the intake on the bottom and a piece of hose leading out. I wired the hose to a thwart so that it pointed over the gunwale. I kept the valve on the bottom of the canoe beside me.

This contraption paid off on its first trip out. In a narrow channel between islands, choppy waves were suddenly breaking over us from several different directions. As fast as we turned to meet one we'd get sloshed from the other side.

At first I thought that my hands were too full for footwork and that it would be unwise to lift my weight from the kneeling position. But too much water was coming in. I eased up to the seat, got a heel on the pump, and, without letting up on the paddle, started stamping. The water shot out in an arc thirty feet long, squirting like a fire hose against a cliff that we were passing. In a few minutes we were out of the cross-waves, wet but riding high. The pump would suck water down to the last inch.

I had seen that device just once in a catalog and had sent for it. It lasted for years. I have never found another like it, although any number of hand- and motor-operated pumps are advertised, all equally worthless in a canoe. Sometimes a really good thing is unable to survive in the bewildering mass of shiny competition. But it was a simple gadget and could be rigged at home.

These measures made us feel more secure. As the years passed and the children grew up we had an increasing feeling of freedom, a sense that we didn't have to be quite so conservative.

I wasn't conscious of being willing to risk my life or my wife. But we began to travel in winds that would earlier have kept us grounded, to cross wider traverses, and sometimes to strike out for an island in the misty distance. As we extended our voyages we got to feel quite safe so long as the wind was steady and the water deep beneath us.

The waves were often enormous in the open lake, but not so tricky as the breakers that stumble over the shallows. Lifted on one of the far-out billows we could see many miles in all directions. At the crest, the bow might move out over empty space where Fay's paddle stroke would miss the water. As our center of gravity went over the edge, the bow would drop with a spanking slap and we would toboggan down the slope. In the trough we could see only the green hills of water towering above us. Then we'd be paddling hard to climb the next one.

These big deep-water waves don't break much into a properly-handled canoe. There is likely to be enough spray to keep the bow paddler soaked, but we could usually avoid having much water slurped into the hull.

Sometimes, even way out in the lake, we'd see a momentary fountain shoot up above the waves. That meant a rock or a reef near the surface. We'd give it plenty of room. If the wind got to veering around we'd head for shore.

A psychiatrist, questioning me about these ventures, tied them in with what he had already decided to be my excessive fear of death.

"All right, old Bones, here we are. Come and get us if you can. See, you're not so all-powerful."

I argued that dying was important enough to deserve a lot of consideration. Look at all the words spilled over it by the poets and philosophers. Almost as many as about love. I didn't think that I was any more scared than they were. Anyway, not to the point of taking steps to hasten my finish. But who was I to enter into debate with the expert?

> Myself when young did eagerly frequent
> Doctor and sage, and heard great argument,
> But ever more found myself brought out
> By that same gate wherein I went.

I suppose that my long-lasting enthusiasm for Omar supports the diagnosis. And there are probably a lot of other disgraceful psychological giveaways in this book. What do I care! Let the doctors and the sages argue that stuff. But nevermore at my expense.

Once a commercial fisherman, pushing his power-dory for shelter from a rising wind, passed us as we were paddling out of the harbor. He pointed his finger at his head and made a whirling gesture. Another psychiatric diagnosis. And similar conclusions have been drawn by others in connection with my environmental activities.

In spite of all this consensus, I'm not admitting that I'm any crazier than the rest of you. Or anyway, not so you can prove it by my paddle-practices.

This is a dangerous world. Whatever you do is risky. If you don't do anything, that's not very safe either. I have often been scared on the water, but the only time that I have been close to death was when I took the authorities' advice and put on that life jacket.

It seems to me that sky-divers, ski-jumpers, mountain climbers, snow machine riders (especially snow machine riders), cyclists, jaywalkers, smokers, drivers who don't fasten their seat belts, and shoppers who buy breakfast cereal without reading the list of ingredients all take greater risks. Those courageous people never quail, or they conceal it if they do. They can't all be crazy.

Chapter 30

FORCED LANDINGS

This mounting wave will roll us shoreward soon.
                                        Tennyson

In 1823 Dr. John Biggsby, a member of the international boundary commission, saw one of the big fur trade canoes driven by the wind against Lake Superior's north shore. Just as it was about to hit the rocks the entire crew went over the side. Some held the boat while others got the baled pelts ashore. Then, all together, they carried the canoe up through the surf beyond the reach of the waves.

I think that I can add some detail, from an experience of ours, to Biggsby's account and maybe reconstruct some of the feelings of the tempest-tossed voyageurs.

Biggsby and his British and American colleagues settled on the Omeemeezeebi, the Pigeon River, as the dividing line. North of its mouth a chain of islands extends some twenty miles at an angle to the shore.

Fay and I were paddling close inside this stringy archipelago, keeping close to its shores, making use of its shelter. A stiff wind was shaking the trees and whipping the surface between the islands.

A stiff wind, but safe. It was coming out of the Southeast. The worst that it could do to us would be to blow us a few miles off our course and set us down on the mainland.

That's how a person will casually discount some possible future emergency. When it really happens, you may not feel so comfortable.

We were crossing one of the openings in the island chain when the wind began to get the better of us. Paddling at full strength we were shipping too much water and not making enough headway. Gradually it became clear that we were not going to get to the next shelter.

So all right, now we go into Plan Two. Swing her down wind and head for the hills.

At about the third stroke in that direction we were caught by the full force of the gale and swept away from all island protection.

The waves banged in from the stern and showered down on us. We picked up speed fast. The canoe began to throw spray out from both sides of the bow like a motorboat. The faraway hills got big. The land came flying at us. White uprisings of surf rolled along its length.

There wasn't much time to study the shoreline. I could see a headland of big rocks standing out, forming a cove. That should mean some kind of a stony beach with a rough but slanted bottom. Better than boulders. We headed for it.

We shouted quick plans. Fifty feet from the breakers I gave the signal. Fay slid over one side and I over the other. But I lingered on the gunwale long enough to partly fill the canoe with water and slow its wind-driven rush.

We hung to it, dragged along fast enough. Our feet were searching for the bottom. When they found it they took a well-braced hold and stopped the canoe.

I got my knife open, cut the bindings, and stumbled ashore with a pack. Its weight gave me a footing on the moss-slippery stones under the water. I waded out, threw my bundle well up on the shore and looked back.

The canoe was jerking and tossing like a doe in a rawhide snare. Fay had to give a little ground but was hanging on, still at a safe distance from the surf.

The return trip was harder. A man is most vulnerable when he's empty-handed in the shallows. That's where the combers get their best whack at him and where there's the least water to break a fall.

I kept low, feeling my way for firm footholds, bracing to meet each wave. There was no stability here without a burden. On the third trip I was knocked down and tossed on the beach like a piece of driftwood.

I'd say that this particular landing was about as rough and confused as a losing game of football, but compressed into fewer minutes. Fay went on holding and I went on carrying. Eventually, all our cargo was lying in a loose pile, a source of little rivers that ran back across the dry rock slanting down into the surge and back flow of the surf.

The first step in getting a canoe out of a lake is to get the lake out of the canoe. You do this by rolling up one side before you lift. The hoist goes better if you're not lifting a boatload of water.

That simple principle is easily forgotten when you're trying to get out quickly before the arrival of the next breaker.

The canoe was dented, the food, blankets and watercolor paper soaked, the people bruised, but nothing seriously damaged. We set up camp, built a fire, hung or spread the wet things to dry, tapped out the dents in the aluminum, and made ourselves comfortable until the weather changed.

The *canots du maitre* of the fur trade were thirty-six feet long and loaded with close to four tons of cargo. The voyageurs would have had to plan and carry out their forced landings far more expertly than we did.

Some of them would have been told off to snatch the bundles out of the bow and stern immediately while others held the canoe. She would have to be carrying most of the load in the middle to ride over the moving fulcrums of the waves without breaking up.

The *bourgeois*, the man in command, would have made sure

that the bales of fur were stacked beyond the reach of the surf. Then he would have run down to supervise the rest of the liftout.

After that, canoe and cargo would be carried farther up to where the spruce gave shelter from the wind. Fires would be built there and the bundles of pelts opened for drying. A party would be sent down to the beach to recover the flotsam: bags, boxes, kegs, bedrolls, and paddles as they washed ashore. The forest would provide bark, planking, fiber, and pitch for repairs.

It was making the best of a bad situation. Men might have been injured or drowned. Worse, in the company's view, valuable furs might have been damaged. When the *bourgeois* got back to Montreal he might face a fine or demotion for having had the bad judgment to travel when he should have laid over.

Men have never been able to predict all the sudden changes that sweep across Lake Superior. Sometimes, but not often, a long canoe was lost with its cargo and crew.

In our own times, when one of the great ore carriers goes down, the men on the other ships will shake their heads and say, "Tough luck." But most of them keep on sailing. I suppose that the fur trade mariners accepted such disasters in the same way.

Chapter 31

WORKING MAN

> Sweet is the memory of past labor.
> Euripides

Rest break. Breathing hard and still sweating in the cool evening air, I leaned on my crowbar. The sun was lighting just the tops of the birches below me, turning the yellow leaves to orange. Beyond, the lake stretched cool and blue to the horizon.

As I stood there watching, a great boulder rose silently from the beach to a height of perhaps thirty feet. It seemed to hang there for a moment. Then I heard the explosion. The rock dropped as though shot down by a marksman.

Men were changing the landscape down there, blasting a harbor from the rock and building a stone causeway to an island.

I had seen the advertisement for workers to build the new taconite plant at Silver Bay. From these towers a river of waste material would flow into Lake Superior. I had written and spoken against this pollution, but our opposition had been overrun by the demand for jobs and business.

My illustrations, portraits and writing, never very enriching, seemed to be particularly out of favor with editors and sitters that fall. We needed cash money. The offer of $1.75 an hour overwhelmed whatever reluctance I felt about working for polluters. Ham and I signed up.

The other men commuted back and forth the sixty miles to Duluth, but we set up our tent in the woods, with Fay to take care of us.

I took the step with some misgivings. My mother considered it unwise: "John's not used to that kind of work." Beryl said, "This will be the first time in my memory that Dad worked on a job where he wasn't the boss."

I felt that I was an impostor, pretending to be a capable construction worker. Would I be able to keep up with younger men, who were also more experienced? Would I be exposed as a fraud and dismissed?

Ham and I were assigned to one of the towers, vast cylinders that were being erected to store the taconite ore. The new crew assembled on the disk that would be its floor. Our job was to keep jacking up the wooden forms that held the wet concrete in place as it hardened into walls.

The foreman explained how this would be done, then looked us over, selecting the first victim. His eye lit on me. I turned my head and looked at the lake.

"You there. The big guy."

I could no longer pretend not to hear.

"Yes, you. Come here."

I took an unwilling step forward. He handed me a crowbar. I inserted it into the socket of the jack as directed, took a deep breath, and bore down on it with all my strength.

Nothing happened.

In shame and desperation I hoisted my weight on the tilted bar. Like in the old days, prying the Ford out of the mud with Chinky.

Slowly, my end of the bar bowed in reluctant surrender. The section of curved wooden form rose squishingly to a higher level.

"Okay," said the straw boss. "Now everybody take a bar."

I had fooled him, but could I last out eight hours of it?

Really, there was nothing to worry about. We worked hard, but had frequent rest breaks. It was no worse than chopping brush on the farm. And nothing like paddling into a 'Tschgumi head wind.

At midnight the next shift took over. Ham and I walked down to the road, only comfortably tired. Fay was waiting for us in the truck. The security men had taken her for a camp follower and tried to chase her off, but she refused to leave.

For the next sixteen hours it was just good October camping: supper cooked on a fire in front of the open tent, late sleep into the morning, some painting along the shore, or by the deep-cut stream that ran close to our camp. Then back to the tower. It was as good as a canoe trip.

The Korean War had ended not long before, and most of our fellow-workers were just out of the army. In the ancient military tradition they were filled with strange oaths.

There seemed to be a grammatical rule that every noun must be preceded by the adjective "fucking."

"Take your fucking hammer and go up the fucking ladder and nail the fucking plank." In that first night on the job I laughed aloud as the picture suddenly hit me of all these articles coming to life in a joyous orgy of copulation. What a crop of miniature equipment they would produce!

At the Boat Club and again at Exeter I had heard more obscenity, delivered with imagination and enthusiasm by young men who were being kept more or less segregated from women. Almost everybody on the taconite towers was married and went home every night. They spoke their lines in a matter-of-fact way, without dramatic expression. The trouble was that it took so long to say anything. It was like waiting for somebody with a severe speech defect to get his statement out when you should be doing something else. But they were friendly and we got along well.

Nowadays, of course, even the most refined ladies use far more colorful language, and so do many pastors.

As our tower grew we had to climb to the working floor by a ladder, and later by a series of ladders running up from one platform to the next. The distance to the ground became intimidating. I learned not to look down, but just to watch the rungs ahead of me as I went up. The saying was that if you fell you would be picked up on a blotter. Nobody fell.

During the rest breaks, rumors were stated with such assurance that, for a while, I believed all of them. I especially favored the one about state law requiring payment of time-and-a-half above the hundred foot level. When we got up beyond that height I was disappointed that my pay check failed to show this increase.

The steelworkers were the aristocrats of the towers. They were paid much more than the rest of us. They climbed like spiders on the swaying rods above us, welding and wiring them into a sturdy web of reinforcement over the rising concrete.

None of these experts happened to be on hand one night when one of their high fastenings gave way. The foreman told Ham to get up there and wire it together.

He started the climb.

I looked over the edge. I had no business to interfere and no authority. Ham was of age. But the ground looked terribly far away.

I called up to him, "No. Come back. I can't let you take that chance."

I didn't know whether he would obey me. I figured that we would both be fired if he did.

He stopped, looked at me, smiled, climbed down.

The foreman shrugged. Somebody else volunteered. The work went on. No reprisals.

We wondered whether we would be camping there all winter. No such luck. One real Minnesota law, not discovered by the rumor-distributors, was that casual labor acquired certain rights after a given time on the job. So one day we were all laid off and a new crew took over. I was sorry. I had enjoyed the work and the life.

Long before this, when I quit my job, I had offered my resignation as a director of the two family banks. My father had refused to accept it. That turned out well for me.

On the second Tuesday of each month I would get into my store clothes and drive to town for the board meetings. The fees, while small by today's standards, were a valued reinforcement to our feeble personal economy. The discussions of loans and of management policies gave a change of pace for a few hours and kept me in touch with goings-on in the banking business.

The years passed quickly in my oddly assorted occupations. When my father died, my mother and my brothers urged me to take over the management of the Proctor bank.

I hesitated. I was getting an increasing number of portrait commissions and was illustrating for several small magazines. For several years Fay, Ham, and I had been publishing *The Magazine of Ducks and Geese*. These projects had become more important to us than farming. We were getting by.

We were also aging without the proper middle-American increase in assets. I went back to the bank.

Contrary to the general belief, there is never a dull moment in that line of work. You sit there like an old hen on a pile of other people's money, trying to hatch something, while various talented individuals do their inspired best to snaggle the dollars out from under you. You watch them with a cold eye and peck off those that you think are unlikely to pay it back.

To make it really difficult, you must accomplish this in the context of a moldering mass of state and federal laws, each designed to frustrate the self-serving trick of some sly banker or to promote that of some wise and foreseeing statesman.

When these regulations have outlived their usefulness nobody bothers to remove them. They are left lying there, rusty booby traps in the weeds, forgotten by everybody except the sharp-eyed bank examiners, who watch them from a distance, ready to pounce. You learn to work your way cautiously around them. Often, even routinely, they prevent you from helping people and business firms that need and deserve financing.

During the depression years banks were going broke all over the place, or being gobbled up by bigger outfits like minnows by a pike. Once you've seen that you can never be entirely convinced that it won't happen again. My aim was to make sure that, when it did, the Proctor bank would live through it again as it did under my father in the thirties.

I have always been an untidy bookkeeper, inaccurate at making change, forgetful of names, faces, and signatures, and an obviously insincere glad-hander and back-slapper. But I have an eye for people who will be good at these and other bankerly accomplishments. I studied the high school honor rolls, discussed the top students with their teachers, and invited the most promising to come in for interviews. Then I would make my choice. With hardly any exceptions, these kids did well. I was able to spend more and more time at drawing and painting—in the studio, the canoe, and the western mountains.

I opened a studio-gallery-art school in Duluth where I showed my work and that of other painters, U.S. and Canadian, who specialized in wilderness subjects.

"*Il faute epater le bourgeois,*" said Beaudelaire. We must shock the money-grubbing middle class. Picasso and other leftists made this the modern artist's creed.

As a banker, the ultimate in bourgeoisie, moonlighting as an artist, or vice-versa, I became aware that each of these groups viewed the other with some contempt and a great deal of suspicion. I tried to keep my activities in one secret from my colleagues in the other. But I could only get away so long with leading a double life. Eventually all concealment broke down.

My cousin, who was president of a bank in Superior, asked me why I didn't retire from banking entirely and spend my full time painting. I answered that I rather liked the variety of going from life among the artists to the bank and spending a few hours in the rational world.

"And which is the rational world?" he wanted to know. That question could well be pondered by today's authorities in art and finance.

Chapter 32

SEARCH PARTIES

> De win' she blow a hurricane
> An 'spose she blow some more
> You can't get drown on Lac St. Pierre
> So long as you stay on shore.
>   William Henry Drummond

The trees spread wide at their tops, shading everything below. The ground was level and almost free of brush, like a big room, empty except for the verticals of the trunks. The new leaves were a pale sap green. Among them were great numbers of little singing birds of the same color as the leaves.

We were sitting in a spot where the spring sunlight found a way down through the foliage. The warmth felt good. The cool wind had been blowing for a long time. It was daring us to put our canoe in the water.

That was a challenge that we would not ordinarily have accepted. We would have been happy to stay in this beautiful place as long as the wind might wish. But I had failed to keep our custom of telling nobody when to expect us back from the woods. Under pressure of business appointments I had promised to return by a certain day. Yesterday. Well, maybe the wind would go down with the sun.

After supper the branches were still swaying overhead. I stood on the beach trying to imagine that the waves were easing a little. Fay came down beside me.

"You're not thinking of going out in that, are you?"

I had been thinking about it, but now it seemed like a poor idea. We went back to camp.

At dawn the wind was still strong.

"We'd better go anyway," I said. "Our kids and our parents are going to be worried by this time. It's only Winnibigoshish, not 'Tschgumi."

Fay studied the waves again before replying.

"Better load the heavy stuff well back in the boat then. We'll have to quarter into the wind. Everything is going to get soaked. Especially me, up in front."

As we left the shelter of the cove, the lake stretched empty before us. No fishing boats out there today. Fay had slipped an old canvas poncho over her head and tied a piece of rope around her waist to hold it down and keep her a little dry. She was paddling hard, and looking ahead. In the stern I was watching the waves as they came in, shifting my weight to tilt the canoe against the occasional big one. Plenty of spray was breaking over the bow, but we weren't shipping much solid water.

It was heavy work. We paddled silently all morning. Toward noon Fay turned her head a little and shouted.

"There's something dark way off in the whitecaps. I think it's a boat."

A little later she called again.

"I saw a paddle flash."

"That's got to be some of our family," I hollered back. "Nobody else would be that crazy."

Sure enough, as we came closer, there were Ham and Norman.

Some person in authority had said, on a basis unknown, that we were on Cass Lake. The boys had spent the night looking for our truck along its shore. By early morning they had started checking the access places on Winnie and had found our pickup at the end of the Raven Point trail.

But out there on the heaving water was no place for small talk.

They turned around and we all dug for the distant landing.

Suddenly from overhead came a roar that drowned out the noise of wind and water. A dark shadow swept down like a hawk on swimming ducks. I stopped paddling and cowered in terror. The canoe veered broadside. A wave swept over the gunwale.

The fighter passed above, then swung around and headed back at us, clearly on a kamikaze mission. Again I was crouching down there trying to dig through the hull.

At the last moment the pilot chickened out and winged off into the sky. By this time the canoe was wallowing in the trough, threatening to capsize at any moment. We went to work, I with the paddle to head it into the wind, and Fay with the bailing bucket. I was trying to fend off each threatening wave and, at the same time, sluing my head around to watch for another air strike.

No more came. At last we splashed up through the surf on the broad sands of Raven Point. Fay drove the car and I the truck, with one of the boys in each. It was like old times, driving home with kids asleep in the back.

As I came to the door of our house I could hear the phone ringing. It took me a while to fumble out the key, but the caller was persistent. I finally got to the screaming instrument and quieted it. Over the line came the stern voice of authority.

"Is this the John L. Peyton residence?"

Timidly, I confessed that it was.

"This is the Cass County Sheriff's office. We've found the boat, floating bottom up. We'll let you know as soon as we have the bodies."

"Well thanks. If there's anything we can do . . .?"

"Not right now. At this point we're taking care of everything."

"Could you tell me who . . . ?"

But the officer had no time for more idle questions.

"We'll keep you informed," she said, and hung up.

Fay had come in and was sliding out of her pack straps.

"What was that about? You look grim."

"There's been a boating accident, a bad one. It must be somebody we know, or they wouldn't be calling us. What boat, I wonder? Whose bodies?"

The phone rang again. It was the *Duluth Herald* wanting to know if there was any news about the Peytons. I said no, nothing unusual that I knew of.

Then it began to get through to me. All this public curiosity was focused on us.

So I was ready for the next call, which came immediately. This time it was from a radio station. The man seemed disappointed to hear that we were both alive, but he said that he would make the best of it anyway, and turned on the tape for an interview.

He was not interested in my statement that we'd just had a pleasant holiday. He wanted to know what had been the most frightening moment. That was easy.

He explained that the plane had been one of several National Guard aircraft sent out to search for us. They hadn't been trying to drown us or scare us to death, but just to find out whether we answered to the description. They had decided that we didn't. That was correct: they had been ordered to find two people, not four.

After that, our going-away statements were definite. "If we never come back it will be because we've decided to stay out there. So don't ever bother to search for us, please."

Chapter 33

VOYAGE ALONG AN ANCIENT SHORE

> The coast between Otter's Head and the River Peek
> ... is more deeply indented than that between the
> former place and the crags. Its hills are higher, more
> massive, and often dip precipitously into woody
> dells. The water-margin is lined with low, jagged
> rocks, while the interior is very barren, the whole
> vegetation being a few small Canada Pines, de-
> formed and apparently dead, save a little pencil of
> leaves at the top.
>
> John J. Biggsby

The road led down between the Ontario hills and through the cool, yellowing hardwoods of late August. It ended at a logging camp on the Pik River.

A rough sign growled at us: KEEP OUT THIS MEANS YOU. We paused, trying to find some friendly suggestion in that brief message.

"Well, it doesn't say YOU SON OF A BITCHES, so let's give it a try."

We stopped in front of the office. A big man, with hat pulled down over his eyes, came out, spat a wad of tobacco juice, tilted back his head, and asked what we wanted.

"We'd like to paddle down toward Otter Head. Can we leave our truck here?"

"Over there by the cook shanty. That will be close to the river. The Chinaman will show you where to park. Need a hand to get your stuff down?"

We assured him that we could manage.

The kitchen was rich with the smell of doughnuts. The cook offered a pan of them for our selection. We each took one but refused the coffee.

"Leave your truck right outside my window," he said. "I can keep my eye on it there. Nobody would take anything but one of the kids might monkey with it."

The canoe rose and fell gently on swells running up the river from the lake. We set the packs, tent roll, axe, and bucket into its hull. This had been dented and tapped out so many times that hardly a smooth spot remained. But, like its owners, it was still in fairly good working order.

When we reached the mouth, surf was breaking over the bar, but we figured that the wind would ease soon. A rugged coast stretched away to the Southeast. Steep promontories stood out into the lake and ended in islets, reefs, and upright needles of rock. Between these points rose palisades, broken down, in some places, into masses of tumbled granite.

Soon this expanse of stone was glowing red in the reflected sunset. The evening was clear and the breeze cool. We began looking for a sheltered place to camp.

We found it in a fiord that ran far back into the hills. A boom of moss-covered logs, lying slack in this calm water, curved across a narrows. We slid over a gap left by its sagging chains. The water inside it was covered with logs. We worked through them, sneaking between some and pushing others out of the way.

Two miles down the bay we landed on a sand beach. The deep, fresh tracks of a bear made me feel like Robinson Crusoe.

During the night we could hear him snuffling and pawing at the kettle for any greasy tidbit that might have been left, but he stayed away from the tent.

In the morning a pair of blue herons were standing against the white mist background. When we got out our sketch pads they flapped into the air and headed out over the bay. Fay called out to them, "Oh please don't go." Obligingly they circled back and went on with their fishing. Goes to show there's no harm to ask.

We drew for a long time, forgetting breakfast. Herons are fine-looking birds and these sketches have since been the basis for several pictures painted back in the studio.

By the time they had left and we had eaten and packed, the sun was high and so was the wind, driving straight at us down the length of the bay. The boom had come to life. The logs were jerking at their chains, straining them tight, leaving us no place to paddle over the connecting links.

At one end, the boom was held by a great iron rod, set deep into the rock. We went ashore here, thinking that we might be able to carry across. But waves were breaking against the lake side of this point. Not too rough to travel, but much too rough to launch.

We sat down for some sketching, but now I was impatient to get on. I closed my pad and stood looking out over the heaving line of logs. The words came without forethought, but earnestly and distinctly.

"I wish that boom would break."

At that moment a mighty wave surged against the barrier. Somewhere out in its plunging length a rusty link gave way. Slowly the long gate swung open.

Coming so soon after the heron recall, it was a little frightening. If I'd realized that I had that much influence, I would have been more careful what I said.

Except for its unwelcoming sign, the logging firm had been good to us. I hadn't intended to sabotage its property. But the next change of the wind would send its logs swimming like ducks out of the bay. And how about our legal liability?

It was too late now for regrets, so we might as well make the most of the opportunity. Fay squatted above a rock basin, holding the canoe with a paddle while I loaded it. Even in this sheltered hollow there was enough lifting and dropping in the water level to make this a tricky operation. One moment the canoe would be at my feet. The next it would be way down below, so that I had to wait, with a pack in my hands, for the next inrush to boost it up within reach again.

When everything was in place we lowered ourselves cautiously, not letting go of the rocks until the hull came pushing up against our feet. We took off our shoes and folded our jackets for kneeling pads.

Being mere white people, we stay on the seats whenever we safely can. The Indian's knee-bone position is not much for comfort, but just right for stability, maximum power, and, in emergency, fervent prayer. We took it now.

As we left the shelter of the chain-draped point the wind struck us full force. We plowed straight into it until we judged that we were far enough out to be clear of any ordinary shallows. Then we turned left along our southerly course.

This put us broadside to the waves, but they were the big, languorous, deep-water variety. The onshore wind assured us that, even if we were to goof, the water would not be too cold and the drift-ride to shore would be fairly speedy.

We went to earth that night where a river ran down into the lake between stone ridges. There was a wide meadow here, with plenty of firewood, blueberries and a good harbor. We stayed for two days, fishing, painting, swimming, and exploring upstream. We ate blueberry bannock, blueberry flapjacks, and blueberries in the oatmeal.

Several times, while smoothing out a painting spot, kneeling to pick berries, or sitting by the fire, we felt hard objects embedded in the mass of old berry vines or the earth beneath us. When dug up these were found to be articles left by earlier campers: a bent spoon or some unidentifiable utensil. We wondered what there might be further down, early copper implements perhaps, or Norse iron. This would have been one of the few good places to come ashore and camp along this coast.

The river meadow is a good place for moose, too. In the morning and evening we saw them pasturing, and during the nights we heard several crash through the brush along the bank and splash down into the river.

We cruised on south in the pleasant condition of having no deadlines to meet, and of being in no hurry to get anywhere.

This state of mind is not easily achieved. When I was young I used to cook breakfast by dim, predawn light, be on the water as the sun rose, paddle and portage all day, and then, beside the fire at night, measure the map to see how many miles had been covered. I missed a lot of good things that way.

We paddled several miles up one river looking for a place to camp. The cedars grew so thick along the bank that we could hardly get through them. At last we climbed in over the curving trunks, cut several of them to make an opening, dragged the cargo through it, and then the canoe.

Next day on the river we met a prospector, the first person we'd seen since leaving the Pik. He told us that if we'd go a couple of miles farther upstream, climb the cliffs and look down into the gorge, we'd see a sight of pickerel.

They were there, all right. Leaning over the edge as far as we dared, we could see, at first, just the white tips of the fins moving in the water below. Then, gradually, we made out the fish, row after row of dark shadows, hanging almost motionless in the swift current.

For some reason I found it necessary to lower a worm on a hook. The fish ignored it except to shift position a little when it bumped their noses. That was just as well. I had no plans as to how I was going to hoist one of those heavyweights all the way up to where we perched on the brink.

There were plenty of the same size walleyes to be caught at canoe level, anyway. Canadians call these fish "pickerel" just as they say "bush" for woods. It makes fish and forest sound runty, but I suppose that's British understatement.

And so we took our leisurely way along this uninhabited coast with its strange stone shapes that stand up along the shore or rise out of the lake like surrealist sculpture. At noon we went ashore and bathed in basins of sun-warmed water that were cooled and refilled from time to time by surges from the deep.

We were not counting the days, but we knew that they were passing quickly. Warming ourselves by the fire one night we agreed that it was time to turn back. We knew that we had been out longer than we had intended and that we were somewhere near the stone formation known as Otter Head, but that was all we were sure of. Food, except for fish and berries, was running low. At night the northern lights flared above the hills and a skim of ice formed on the water bucket. Fall can be a stormy season along the north shore, and we had to consider the possibility of being forced ashore by wind and held there for an indefinite time.

But with a clear sky the next morning, and a brisk northwest breeze to speed us along, we decided to go on for one more day. It always seems important to round another palisaded cape, or to find out what's beyond those islands.

It rained that night and kept on raining for the next two days, a cold, driving torrent sideswiping in from the Northeast. We didn't mind. Our tent was freshly waterproofed and we were warm in our down sleeping bags. We took turns reading aloud between intervals of sleep.

When the rain let up we crawled out for a look around. The land here, if you could speak of it as land, consisted of granite slabs, some lying flat and some upended, covered with thick moss. We climbed, not easily, a steep hill of this stuff and came out on a far-reaching view of points, wooded islands, and the wave-battered little islets of barren rock that the Norsemen, if they came this way, called skerries. It was still too windy to travel, and we spent the afternoon up there, sketching and watching the storm blow itself out.

The next day we started back toward the North. Again we had a wind quartering behind us. We paddled hard down the face of each big swell, trying to stay on its forward slope as long as we

could before the crest ran out from under the canoe and left us to be picked up by the next one.

Turning into a river mouth at sundown we found a large boat, a yacht, really, anchored inside the sandbar. Three boats were just getting back to it from fishing, with big catches. We were invited aboard for dinner. A camera was brought out to record the occasion.

Our hosts were business and professional men from Detroit who had been getting together every summer to make this fishing cruise. Each time, when they got home, they had been telling their wives about the beautiful women they met up here in the woods. Now they would have the proof.

As we came alongside the dock on the Pik, a group of loggers walked down to meet us. They seemed to have assumed responsibility for our safe return. They told us that if we hadn't come in that evening they'd have been out looking for us the next day.

Chapter 34

THE NOISE OF A CRUSADE

> After he has eaten a thousand mice
> the cat goes into a monastery.
> Tibetan proverb

Returning from the forest with long hair, tattered clothing and skin burned dark, I have several times been mistaken for an Indian. These errors happened a long time ago, when Indians looked like that. On each occasion I felt immensely flattered. And once we fooled an old master.

Fay, Ham, and I were paddling down Rainy Lake, looking for a place to camp on our last night out. Fay's blond hair was covered with a red bandana. The food sack was empty, the canoe was light, and we moved fast over the quiet, evening water.

We heard a shout from the Canadian side. A little, white-haired man was capering on a point there. A boat was pulled up beneath him.

He beckoned to us. We swung in and coasted along the shore, looking up at him inquiringly.

As we approached he stared at us in surprise. Then he explained that he had mistaken us for some Indian friends that he had been expecting. He had crossed the lake to flag them down and had brought some ice cream, which he now invited us to share.

After a long cruise on camp rations, that sounded good. But we wondered whether his other guests might yet appear.

He assured us that they would not be traveling any later in the evening than this. It didn't take a lot of urging.

He introduced himself as Ernest Oberholzer. That name had no particular meaning to me. Just good solid German.

Which shows how negligent I had been about events of great importance to me and to everybody else, then and in years to come, who would paddle over these boundary waters.

Ernest Oberholzer, along with Sig Olson, Bill Magie, and a few others, had fought off a scheme to build a series of dams, flood the country, and log the timber. These men were environmental paladins in the twenties, a time when money was everything and nature was nothing.

For years they held out against the political influence of the paper company and the bitter hostility of their fellow citizens in the border communities who had been sold on the idea that the project would put money into their pockets. If Oberholzer and his colleagues had weakened, or even eased up a little in their struggle, the unique Minnesota-Ontario canoe country would now be as developed and commercialized as are the Black Hills, the Nipigon River, the Wisconsin Dells, or the Florida keys—to name just a few examples of the degradation of magnificent natural resources.

I meant to keep this chapter cool, and already my emotions are showing. But that's the way we are up here in the woods. If we take the slightest interest in these arguments we become passionate partisans of one side or the other.

The conservationists are called un-American, communists, pacifists, cultists, bovine intellectuals, effeminate elitists, posie-sniffers, duck-huggers, homosexuals, and sentimental old ladies. I didn't invent any of those terms of endearment. They have all been used freely by the loyal opposition.

On the other hand, members of the Minneapolis Sierra Club, venturing north for a public hearing, may view the jeering crowd of pro-development locals as something like those other locals in a modern southern novel: shaggy, boozy, unwashed rednecks, ready for any sort of aggression including rape, and not awfully particular about the sex of the victim.

City people who have been donating their time and money for the defense of upstate areas, and who come to those areas expecting the support of the residents, are often taken aback by the zeal and unanimity with which those residents oppose their efforts.

Many of the local people enjoy hunting, fishing and camping. They claim, with apparent sincerity, to love the country and to be taking good care of it. Why, then, do they fight every attempt to protect the woods, water, and wildlife, while they back each proposal that would reduce or destroy them?

I think that I can offer an explanation of what conservationists call "the redneck reaction," because I've always been a redneck, and, in early years, a rather extreme and obnoxious example. As the decades passed I didn't like the new restrictions on wilderness behavior, nor their tightening enforcement.

Not that they made so much difference to me. I began shooting when it was light enough to see the ducks against the sky. A shorter legal hunting season didn't reduce my hunting season. A chain barrier across a road was an invitation to chain-saw a detour around it. This was all in the frontier tradition: very American.

I must have read in the papers about Oberholzer, but I hadn't been paying enough attention even to recognize the name when I heard it there on the Canadian rocks. I was taking everything I wanted and contributing nothing.

It took a direct attack on my own selfish interests to bring me into alliance with the environmentalists. The proposed extension of an interstate highway would pass through a lakeshore park and continue beside Lake Superior, bringing noise and air pollution to a long expanse of shoreline within the Duluth city limits and promoting suburban sprawl over the wooded area beyond them. But what got my attention was that it would also take my studio-gallery.

I went to an anti-freeway gathering, liked the people I met there, and signed up for the duration.

The city government, the state and federal highway administrations, Duluth business and labor organizations, the newspapers, and the television stations were united in their determination to put the road through regardless of opposition. To accomplish this, the advice of consulting engineers and city planners was disregarded, public hearing results were falsely reported, and "citizens' committees" were shamelessly loaded.

When demand for a vote on the project could no longer be disregarded, a "freeway referendum" was presented to the voters with no place on the ballot for a vote against the freeway. The results were quoted all the way from St. Paul to Washington as evidence that Duluth people were strongly in favor of the project.

My file folder, where reports of this and similar sly maneuvers are stored, is labeled DIRTY TRICKS. They probably all seemed legitimate strategy to the people on the other side. To them, I-35 was a great, patriotic cause, for the ultimate glory of God and Duluth, an end that justified any means.

I was so outraged that, for several years, I neglected both my art and my business to "work on the highway." My gallery became the headquarters for the Stop the Freeway Citizens Action Group.

It was a typical environmental crowd, mostly liberals but including a few of us reactionaries. Such organizations are always in danger of being wrecked on the reefs of diverse opinions. With restraint on both sides, we managed to avoid discussion of our political and ideological differences until we knew each other well enough to josh about them.

This experience in opposing the establishment opened my eyes to the many other actions that are always being carried out to exploit natural resources for somebody's quick profit at the expense of everybody else. And particularly at the expense of those generations who, not having yet been born, can't speak for themselves.

No moralist is so unrelenting as the reformed sinner. Having carried out my own depredations, I was eager to prevent young poachers from getting their share. Or, to put it more favorably, having enjoyed the forest, I wanted others to go on enjoying it into the distant future.

I became involved in efforts to establish a national park in the Rainy Lake area, to limit motor use and logging in the boundary waters, to designate two forest rivers for government protection, and to tighten state and federal regulations against the pollution of air and water.

In conflicts of this nature, the leaders of society, as well as of business, labor, and politics, usually stand with the developers. Some of the fights get rough.

As an elderly banker siding with flaky leftists against the right-thinking people, I made a good target. I could smile at the disparaging comments reported back to me. "Eccentric" was the mildest of these. For some of my associates who lost their jobs or were dropped by friends or threatened into silence, it was no laughing matter. Anyone enlisting for environmental combat should make sure that he is not vulnerable to political, social, or economic counterattack. Or else that he doesn't give a damn.

These experiences have made me grateful to those of my pro-progress friends who have remained my friends even after we have verbally clouted each other in print or at public hearings. I never could be sure, on meeting somebody who had been my adversary in such an exchange, just what the reaction would be. Some gave me a chilly greeting and some cut me dead.

My words and actions irritated so many people that I could not possibly be mad at all of them. Or, indeed, any of them. So it's always gratifying to me when, on meeting again, we can just greet each other and talk as though nothing had happened.

Good people and good arguments can be found on both sides, and neither is entirely innocent of loose reasoning and equivocation. But the money is always on the side of exploitation and profit. That's what it takes to hire public relations experts and lawyers who specialize in environmental work.

These analyze the situation and prescribe measures to win over the local people: radio and television broadcasts, newspaper articles and editorials, leaflets, posters, bumper stickers, and home visits by professional smooth-talkers. The developers have made great progress in the art of winning hearts and minds. When adequate profits are in sight, they can establish a majority in any country area or small city and often in an entire state.

As soon as the votes and money are clearly on the same side, state and local politicians hesitate no longer. They charge forward as leaders, shouters, and flag-wavers. Soon the entire community is brainwashed pure and clean. In many cases, not a single citizen will question the decision for destruction.

The occasional exceptions can be inspiring.

At a hearing in Ely, Minnesota, many of the townsmen came unshaven, dressed in woolen shirts, caulked boots, and trousers stagged lumberjack style, with long bowie knives sheathed on their belts. Outside the hall a stuffed figure, dangling by the neck from a logging crane, bore a sign, "Sierra." Inside, the audience was screaming and booing as Sig Olson, woodsman, guide, high school

teacher, writer, and Ely resident, stood up to speak.

He was old, then, and frail. He smiled and moved his spread hands in soothing gestures, gradually quieting his fellow citizens. When he had established some degree of order he opened with conciliatory words. Then he went on into a powerful and well-reasoned address that must have shaken the convictions of many.

On a strictly local issue, where enough money is at stake to justify the expense of a full-scale public relations campaign, the conservationists can almost never win the decision. But they may delay the development for a long time, sometimes long enough to kill it.

When the question is to be decided on a national level they stand a better chance. Most Americans seem to be skeptical of claims that pollution control or the establishment of a protected woodland will bring big increases in taxes or utility rates or the loss of jobs. These threats have been used so fluently and with such disregard for facts that they have lost much of their effect. And even a few residents of a forest area writing or speaking for conservation can be influential in demonstrating that local sentiment is not unanimously pro-development.

The trouble is that, unlike the exploiters' professionals, environmental activists don't get paid for their work. Even when you start with a soundly selfish motive, as I did with the freeway, you soon find that you have spent more time and money and have angered more customers than your interest justifies.

Going beyond that point is what we kids used to call "working for Jesus." In a surprisingly similar figure of speech, renaissance scholars spoke of the Christ-fool, a Parsifal in search of the grail. Lacking that religious faith, most modern crusaders can stay in the fight only so long. Then we return to our own pursuits or to quiet senility, and others must either take up the struggle or allow the birthright to be stolen.

Fortunately, there always seem to be a few more fools.

Chapter 35

DESERT AND SEA

> My spirits infallibly rise in proportion to the outward dreariness. Give me the ocean, the desert, or the wilderness. In the desert, pure air and solitude compensate for want of moisture and fertility.... There is a keen enjoyment of mere animal existence.
>
> Thoreau

I had been painting all afternoon in that dark canyon in the Dragoon Mountains that had once been the fortress of the Apache leader, Cochise. Many war parties had ridden out of its narrow mouth to raid the settlements or the soldiers and had later returned to its safety. The vertical walls and commanding crags provided concealed positions for hundreds of riflemen. Throughout the long Apache wars, this natural fortress was never taken by the U.S. Army.

A hundred years earlier my life wouldn't have been worth a spent cartridge in that place. But I was the only inhabitant that day, and it was darkness, not Indians, that put an end to my work. I would come back here the next morning. I drove down the road looking for someplace nearby where I could spend the night.

A group of ranch buildings off in the rocks and mesquite caught my eye. I drove in and asked if they could put me up for the night. They could, and—noticing my license—there were other people from Minnesota there. Name of Jacques.

"Not Francis Lee Jacques, the artist?" Yes, that was who.

For many years I had admired and studied his landscapes and wildlife work. Along with Winslow Homer's watercolors and the oils of Tom Thomson, they had influenced me more than any other North American art.

Jacques had been working on the Duluth, Missabe and Iron Range Railroad at the same time that I had been demonstrating against it. He would have been climbing poles for the power company in Duluth when I was a kid there, but we had never met.

Later I had been dazzled by a show of his oils and drawings. By that time he was famous and traveling in distant parts of the world to gather material for his museum diorama backgrounds.

So it was my good luck to stumble into the Triangle T in the Arizona valley called Texas Canyon, where Lee and his wife, Florence, were spending the winter.

Ranches in that area were shifting from livestock to humans. Guests were more profitable than cattle in those desert mountains, if somewhat more difficult to handle. The Triangle T was the kind of a place where the eight or ten boarders ate with the family, and where you had to check the bill carefully, when you left, to make sure that they had charged you enough.

The ranch had been discovered by a number of interesting people, including several painters, poets, and writers, who kept it filled to its small capacity. Because of their average age they spoke of it as the nursing home. But conversation was lively at table and around the fireplace at night.

In those years, at the end of each summer season, I would close my gallery, pack as many prints and paintings as my small truck would carry, and drift south and west, stopping along the way to paint and to peddle pictures.

Westerners had more money than common people and more artistic patriotism. From Kansas City on, anything depicting western life, western landscapes, or western history sold better than north woods pictures ever did in Minnesota. And there were lots of fine subjects in the mountains and the desert. So this annual milk run, placing work at galleries and calling back each year with a new supply, worked out pretty well.

That kind of art business is like running a gill net— it must be tended regularly. I had to make sure that my works were properly displayed. If I didn't keep checking they tended to sink into basement storage. Or they might be sold without anybody's getting around to send me the payment. This was usually the result of negligence rather than dishonesty, but either way, if I didn't call regularly, I was likely to lose.

I enjoyed these annual migrations to the Southwest and, later, to the Gulf and the Everglades. Even where the country along the highways had been so commercialized as to offer nothing of interest I could always find side roads that degenerated pleasantly into trails and finally into nothing, taking me back to woods, mountains, desert, swamp, or whatever other wasteland still held out against the degrading embrace of civilization.

My truck was equipped with a winch, and that makes a coward brave. When I got hopelessly bogged down in ooze or hung high on a boulder with all four wheels spinning, I would shut off the motor and start ahead on foot, carrying the hook and dragging the cable behind me. I was always able to find a rock or tree to tie to. Then I'd get back in the cab, put the winch in gear, and feel myself being slowly but irresistibly dragged off or out of whatever was holding me. The truck might be covered with mud or limping from minor injuries, but it always got me back to the unclean but welcome embrace of civilization.

One winter I rented a studio in Tucson and went to work on a series of watercolors dealing with the spectacular history of southern Arizona. This included research at libraries and sketching artifacts in museums, but most of my time was spent on the flat desert floor or in the mountain passes that had been the scenes of the northern push of Mexican colonists and of the Apache wars. That was how I came to Cochise's stronghold and the Triangle T.

I knew that I was on to something good here. I drove back to town, loaded up paints, pictures, and portfolios, and moved to the ranch for the rest of the winter.

This was to be the last year of Lee's life. He was cheerful and seemed to be in good health, but Florence evidently had other information. She was careful of him, always watching to make sure that he didn't overdo.

He was not painting, but they would often come out with me for the day, the Jacques resting in the sun while I worked. It was hard to get Lee to criticize the faults in a picture, but what comments he did make were valuable.

In looking over work that I had brought out from Tucson we came across some nudes. Lee remarked that he had never done one of those. I was amazed. Every "self-taught" artist that I had ever checked up on, at least every good one, had done some time in an art school. Even Charlie Russell, the wild cowboy painter, had studied art in St. Louis during his early youth.

The public seems to feel that self-taught artists must be better, or in some way more admirable, than the factory product. That's why the art school backgrounds are denied by promoters. When you talk to the painters themselves, they tell you.

Like Winslow Homer, Lee had had some instruction from another artist but had not attended art school.

Another friend at the ranch, in her seventies but still vivacious and attractive, used to accompany me on some sketching trips. One evening, by the fireside, this association became the subject of teasing that seemed to get through to my companion.

She drew herself up proudly and said, "I have never made a practice of robbing the cradle."

I was sixty-two at the time, but she wasn't fooling. It all depends on your point of view.

At the end of the winter Beryl joined me. We drove down the west coast highway of Mexico. Between this road and the sea lay a savage but beautiful desert, some twenty to thirty miles wide except at the port cities of Guaymas and Mazatlan. Where we found passable trails through this strip we camped beside the salt water.

This is shown on the map as the Gulf of California. It was called the Sea of Cortez until the conquistadors stopped being heroes and became imperialists. It would be hard to find a shore more different from that of Lake Superior, but it has the same combination of waves, solitude, and stony wilderness.

At some points the mountains rise straight out of the water, gray and barren except for tall green cactus. The only person we saw on the beach was a donkey-driver picking up driftwood. The sea was empty of shipping.

One evening, having turned down a winding little road toward

the shore, we saw a river on one side. It looked like a good place to camp. We drove down through low vegetation to reach it.

I should have known that the spiny desert stuff would hit back. We were setting up the tent when I heard a wheezing sound from the truck. Two of the tires were quietly expiring.

We flung our gear into the box and took off. We made it back to the road, but were halted there by deflation.

What to do next? Warnings came to mind about the speed and thoroughness with which a disabled car would be stripped by the bandito folk of these desert mountains. Indeed, there were some of them now, small ones, peering down at us from their ambush on a cactus-covered butte.

Behind them I made out a sort of dwelling or camp-farm, a thatched roof supported by poles and inhabited by goats, chickens and people. I couldn't see whether these last were armed with guns, bows, or blowpipes. They must be concealing their weapons.

I walked toward them hoping to negotiate a reasonable ransom. A mustached man, resembling the photographs of Pancho Villa, rose from the group under the canopy and swaggered toward me.

"*Buenos noches, Señor.*" Good evening, sir. "*Esta es su casa.*" This house is yours. Can I be of service to you?

My recently acquired smattering of Spanish enabled me to understand this greeting and to feel properly relieved by it, but not to answer its question.

I led him back to the truck, pointed to the tires, and, with gestures and a few words from my Berlitz book, asked that a watch be kept on the crippled thing during our absence. Reassured by his smiles and *si*'s we started the long walk toward the nearest town.

We had gone only a short distance when a car pulled up beside us, its passengers crowding together to make room for us. They drove some distance out of their way to get us to a bus line. We couldn't make out much of what they were saying but it was all very friendly until we got out and I made the mistake of taking some currency from my wallet.

The driver was insulted. I didn't have to know the language to understand, from the chilly tone of his comment, that they had not been transporting us for profit. I put my pesos back in my pocket. They drove away.

An incident like this may startle you if you are used to the cities of the border, where every kind of professional has gathered to separate the fool from his money. You may meet such rapacious types anywhere in Mexico, as in any other country. But when you get past the thievish boundary belt, most of the people seem to want to help a stranger rather than to swindle him. I am told that this derives from both Spanish and Indian traditions of hospitality.

When I came back the next day with a repair truck I took out a ten-peso note, a little over a dollar, and handed it cautiously to the bandit chief. He motioned it away with verbal protest.

The garage man explained that he was not refusing payment but only saying that the amount was excessive. I insisted and he accepted. Ah, those rich gringos! I savored this new sensation of feckless, irresponsible munificence.

Since I have spoken patronizingly about the timidity of visitors in the north woods, my equally far-fetched fears of danger in southern hills and jungles will be noted.

And not just the peril of brigands. Reading up on Mexico, I had been impressed with the variety and potency of its serpents. We came equipped with a snake-proof tent having a sewn-in floor and zippered netting, a type that I despise in canoe country.

As we got down into the tropics we saw brightly colored snakes slither across the road. We also saw local people walking barefoot. It was the same situation, I suppose, as with bears at home. Yes, one might bite you, but the odds against it were so great that there really wasn't any use bothering with precautions. I wore my big boots around camp for a night or two, then went in shoeless comfort like everybody else.

We drove from San Blas down a trail beside the beach and tied our tent between coconut palms. Swimming was fun in the warm surf. We spent a long time in the water. We wondered a little about sharks, but I assured Beryl, on the authority of my book, that there would be none here, in the shallow water.

While we were breaking camp a battered old pickup came bumping along the shore road. Something shiny projected floppily from both sides. As it passed we could see an enormous hammerhead shark bound across the truck box, head sticking out on one side and tail on the other. One of the local boys had caught it just beyond the next bend.

Chapter 36

WINDING DOWN

> In the woods . . . a man casts off his years as the snake his slough.
> Emerson

Like the snake, he can repeat that trick for many summers. When, after a long time in the city, he moves again over the water, he knows that everything is in order.

His responsibilities are simple and immediate. He must find a place to sleep, get something to eat, keep dry and warm through the night. Cold, hunger, and exhaustion dispel business worries and personal problems. Accumulated guilt feelings give way to small, physical discomforts. He can do something about those.

When at last he sits sheltered from wind and rain, with a pile of firewood within reach and supper roasting over the embers, life is good again, untroubled, just as it was when he was young.

But all good things must come to an end. As the years pass, the canoe gets heavier, the portages steeper, the ground more flinty to sleep on.

One by one, I accepted the amenities that I had earlier scorned. The bed of shaped earth gave way to an air mattress, the 4-point Hudson's Bay blanket to a goose-down sleeping bag, the axe to a chain-saw, the canvas jacket to a fur-lined parka.

Each of these good things brought a new lease on my forest life. But each added weight and reduced mobility.

So I found helpers.

The one virtue of my kind of arthritis is that it spreads slowly. People complain about slow diseases, but I'm in no hurry.

Gradually my camp chores, like my business responsibilities, were taken over by younger people. My grandchildren became my Indians. They carried the canoe to the water, put the packs and the tent roll into it, held the gunwale and steadied my elbow while I stepped stiffly down. Then they took positions in the bow and the stern. I sat in the center, helping with the paddle only when the wind was strong, but always supplying plenty of instructions. They cleared the camp site, set up the tent, and cooked supper while I criticized from a folding camp-stool, with cushion.

Now, as my joints stiffen further, I find myself content to go out for the day and sleep in a bed at night. I often drive up the shore to stay with Norm and Beryl. From their house on a hill I can see, in clear weather, the Apostle Islands on the other side of the lake. There is a lot of good landscape painting by the water and in the high places, and I still have adventures.

Sometimes we drive around by a Canadian road to a lake on the border where a friend's island cabin is available. We get to it in Norm's boat with outboard (yes, that's the word) towing a canoe. My arms still work fairly well, so later I paddle out in the canoe and paint from it.

There is a certain point, which I remembered from the time Fay and I came through this chain of lakes on our honeymoon, where tall cliffs rise straight out of the water. I was painting a watercolor of these cliffs and dipping my brush in the lake when it slipped through my fingers. It was a fine big, chisel-edged Siberian sable, with a plastic handle. A wooden-handled brush floats, but this improved modern article was just a little heavier than water. It sank slowly until it came to rest on the top of a boulder that rose into dim light from the surrounding darkness.

I keep a piece of wire in my sketch box for cleaning out the fixatif sprayer. I wrapped this around a pole, bent a hook in it, pushed it down there, and sneaked up on the brush with it.

Leaning far over, I could just reach the brush. It was lively now, in its Asiatic way, unwilling to be snared again. Each time that I got it started up, it would slip out of the hook and come to rest a little farther down the slope of the rock.

So I leaned a little farther.

I leaned too far. The lake came in.

In this kind of a situation there is a point of no return, and I was past it. If you try to regain your balance then, the canoe will capsize. To avoid this I dropped over the side, allowing the canoe to right itself.

The month of May is still early spring on these border lakes. The ice is not long gone and the water is cold.

I tried to climb into the half-flooded boat. I had once considered this an easy trick. Now I was unable to scramble up over the high stern. When I shifted the attempt to a lower point along the gunwale it dipped to the surface.

I frogged the canoe to shore. Not really very far, but it seemed to take a long time. I crawled up on the rocks and splashed carefully back to the boat, my teeth chattering. I emptied my sketch box, used it to bail the water out, repacked the box, and paddled back to the cabin.

By the time I was dry and warm it was too dark to go out again. Next day the brush was gone, washed off the rock, I suppose, and out of sight in deep water.

So old age doesn't guarantee good judgment, and that's not the only example.

Three of my grandchildren and I were paddling downstream. Todd was in the bow, Terry and Lisa amidships. I had taken the stern again, figuring that none of the kids had done enough canoeing in fast water.

The river ahead split itself around an island, with a "sweeper" overhanging the right and deeper side. This is a sagged-down tree that leans out from the bank over the water.

The children called for the left fork, but I, being wiser and more experienced, didn't want to chance the unknown shallows there. I swung the boat to the right, confident that I could maneuver around the tree.

The current was stronger than I had thought, and I was weaker. We were swept toward the sweeper, which reached out for us and flipped us neatly over.

The boys got the boat and the pack to shore. A jacket of mine was floating downstream, and Lisa struck out after it. It had too much of a start. It rounded a bend and I called her back.

When the canoe had been emptied and reloaded we started

downstream again, paddling fast to catch up with the jacket before it should get waterlogged and sink.

By noon we had given that up. We landed on a sandbar, had another swim, made a fire, and roasted some sausages. After lunch we were sitting on a log, looking out over the river, when here came the jacket, still floating high and sassy. It was retrieved, leaving me unpunished for my navigational sin.

⊗⊗

I have stopped giving lessons in drawing and painting because they were getting to be too much like work. But I did put on a pastel demonstration for a very exclusive audience.

The U.S. and Canadian customs stations have been moved several miles down the Pigeon River to the new highway, and the old bridge has been demolished. No smuggling over that one now, and none of those Canuck wetbacks coming across dry.

The paved road that leads to it gets very little traffic and no maintenance. The blacktop is crumbling into a network of cracks and potholes. Some sections have been hoisted by frost, and others dropped below the surface. This ruin, like an old logging camp, inspires a pleasant melancholy and a confidence that the forest will not take long to reclaim its own.

I stopped my truck where a valley dropped away below the road and then stretched on to cliffs that rose cool above the autumn foliage on the far side of the river.

I hung my camp stool and light pack of pastels on my shoulder, and hobbled and caned my way to what seemed the best view. Once having started work, I became so engrossed, as anybody does when painting in such a place, that I lost track of time and of what was going on around me.

When, finally, I had finished the picture and come back to earth, I had a strong feeling that I was being observed. I swiveled around on my stool. A bear was sitting there, ten feet behind me, watching intently.

I felt that I should hand him the chalk and say, "Now you try it. Work with the clean point, don't smooch it, and keep it simple."

But he was only looking. He got up and walked off into the woods.

Chapter 37

WINDIGOG

> Dark behind it rose the forest
> Rose the black and gloomy pine trees
> Rose the firs with cones upon them:
> Bright before it beat the water,
> Beat the clear and sunny water
> Beat the shining Big-sea-water.
>
> Longfellow

Much has been taken since those lines were written, and Longfellow was retelling old tales. But much remains.

That first time I jolted down to the bay of the long portage, the ridges around it had been stripped bare. Flat, gray lichen clung to the boulders. In the boggy strip between the hills and the lake, a stubble of spindly brush stuck up, like whiskers on a dirty face. That was all. The loggers had not left a tree.

'Tschgumi, the Big-Sea-Water, beat bright as it had before the wigwam of Nokomis. The daughter of the moon was gone, and her descendants had covered their lodge poles with tarpaper instead of birch bark. The people looked as skinny and ragged as the vegetation. There was nothing to hunt in the naked hills.

It's different now. The points of spruce and pine rise dark again along the ridges, behind a tracery of pale birch and aspen. The paper-covered wigwams have been replaced by neat buildings, many of government issue. The Indians who live in them are heavier than those in my old memories. Most of them dress, talk and think just like the rest of us.

But some of them have not forgotten their *Iliad*, the stories of daring deeds and self-sacrifice by Anishinabe heroes in the hundred years' war against the Sioux. A few old men and women still tell about demons, demigods, ghosts, talking animals, and witchcraft.

And about windigog.

These are malevolent beings, more feared, more horrible than anything in European mythology. Because they are not all myth. There were some real windigog back there among the smoky legends.

To a hunting people, cannibalism is the unforgivable sin. In the terrible dreams of famine winters, the windigo, the murderer who ate the flesh of his victims, was a nightmare figure.

A cold and hungry stranger coming out of the forest would be given a place by the fire and a share of whatever food might be available. But family members would take turns keeping awake through the night, standing watch in case he should be a windigo.

The real killer-cannibals, probably few in number, were multiplied by rumors and stories into a ghastly throng of evil spirits who hunted people in the forest and under the water.

If dark powers guarded the country north of 'Tschgumi in pagan days, they have been just as diligent against Christian men. This ground is not easily broken, nor long held in submission.

An immigrant from Sweden, Norway or Finland chopped out an opening in the trees, built a cabin, and sent back to the old country for a woman. Together they widened the clearing, pried out and piled up the rocks, planted potatoes, cabbages, and rutabagas, and raised a family.

They acquired a horse, a cow, chickens. They cleared and plowed more fields for hay and oats.

As the young people grew up they were likely to leave for places where the living was easier. A son or a daughter might have stayed on, usually a bachelor or an old maid, taking care of the parents, extending the tenure for one more generation.

Finally this last inhabitant is taken away to a nursing home. By then the brush is moving into the pastures. Soon, nothing remains of the homestead but crumbling log walls and a few lilac bushes and apple trees that may cling to life for some years before they are strangled by the wilderness. The only permanent memorials are the great piles of stones that stand in the forest, to be viewed with awe by an occasional hunter or fisherman from some less resolute culture.

My own land, the acres that I once cleared with axe, mattock, and sweat-slippery pry bar, is well along toward that condition. I stumble over a rusty artifact, push and tear the weeds away from it, and remember selecting it, after long consideration, as a vital piece of equipment. A woodchuck whistles at me from a rock pile to warn me that I am trespassing. The old barn, many times patched and repaired, must soon follow the neighbors' farm buildings into the grass.

The days of railroad building are over. No longer are cuts blasted through rock and tracks laid to strategic and profitable locations. Instead, towns are created out of plastic and supplied by air. They are comfortable, even luxurious, but temporary. Winter roads for tractor-trains follow the frozen waterways as closely as possible. No path could be more transitory than these.

When the mines, logging camps, or other centers of industry

are no longer profitable, they are promptly abandoned. Aspen, alder, birch and hazel brush come in fast, but salable timber grows slowly in this soil and climate. Few of those who first clear-cut an area will be alive to harvest its second crop of timber.

Locomotives once hauled trains of saw-logs down from the hills and out on an enormous concrete pier at the mouth of the Knife River, to be dumped into Lake Superior and rafted to the mills. When I was a child, the timber had all been cut, and the tracks were torn up and removed.

The pier stood for a long time. Fay and I used to set up our easels on it to paint wave studies. As the years passed, gaps were torn out by storms, leaving it a lovely, ruinous landscape subject itself. It's all gone now except a few jagged chunks cast up on the shore. Within a mere human lifetime the lake has shown that it can cleanse itself of man's structures as effectively as can the forest.

The old Indian trails, too, are fading. A few years ago, I drove over the border with Lisa past Lake Nipigon and as far north as the dwindling road would take us. There we put our canoe into a many-legged lake that ran far back into the bush. At one time its long bays and the rivers that enter them provided links connecting heavily used canoe routes. But only we and the loons were cruising over the surface.

We had a week to fish, paint, and explore its channels and islands, but we were unable to get beyond it. We could just trace the vestiges of old portages. The bushes grew thicker in their paths than in the woods through which they passed. In my younger years I might have put the canoe on my shoulders and pushed through them, while saplings bent and sprang back, beating noisily on the hull. Not any more.

Surprisingly, modern machinery and social practices have lowered the population in large areas of Canada instead of increasing it. Outboard motors and snow machines speed travel over the level waters that extend out from road-ends but are not often seen in the back country where gasoline must be portaged.

This equipment, along with schools, welfare payments, and jobs, has drawn wilderness people, Indian and White, in toward civilization. Hunger no longer drives families to isolated hunting camps in the winter woods. The Indians, once said to be a vanishing race, are more numerous than ever. But those of them who go into the deep woods for commercial fishing now charter float planes instead of traveling by canoe. Ice and groceries are delivered by air, and fish come out the same way. Who cares that the ancient portage trails are being taken back by the jungle?

So, for right now, the boreal forest seems to be holding its own against progress. My lifetime has stretched across a century of violence as masses of men surged against each other, fighting for space in a desperately overcrowded planet. But the cold, beautiful wilderness of the Canadian shield rests in quiet balance. Life and death go on in good order without management by government or civilization. A tree that dies, or an animal, or a man, goes into other forms of life or is dissolved and stored in the mother earth.

New dangers are moving in. Air-born gases from distant traffic and industry may be doing evil things to trees as well as to fish, birds, crops and people. And there are other powers now, stronger and more malignant than windigog, that threaten all life.

We can hope that the forest will survive these assaults too, even if we smart animals don't. Maybe, in the coming centuries, dark pines will still rise behind bright water, survivors in a peaceful world.